Cheiro's Guide To The Hand

CHEIRO

COSIMOCLASSICS

NEW YORK

Cheiro's Guide To The Hand
Cover © 2007 Cosimo, Inc.

For information, address:

Cosimo, P.O. Box 416
Old Chelsea Station
New York, NY 10113-0416

or visit our website at:
www.cosimobooks.com

Cheiro's Guide To The Hand was originally published in 1900.

Cover design by www.kerndesign.net

ISBN: 978-1-60206-236-8

The square hand is the most practical and logical of all the types; people with such hands are orderly and practical, more on account of their love of habit and custom than through their real sense of the fitness of things.

——from Chapter II: "The Seven Types of Hands"

ARGUMENT

IF we would have the rest of mankind believe in what we believe in ourselves, then we should place the facts of whatever those beliefs may be in such a clear and candid way, that the veriest sceptic is at least forced to respect such facts.

In this argument—which must necessarily be a short one—I shall endeavour to carry out this principle.

My experience in this work has taught me that people are only sceptical because they *do not know*. There may be some, no doubt, who are willing to take things on faith, but the vast majority of mankind must have facts to appeal to their reason and intelligence.

There are many buried truths in this world of ours ; gold has to be dug and delved for, and so has truth. The dust from Time's chariot wheels has hidden beneath the accumulation of centuries thoughts and things that we are continually stumbling across, and then wondering at our ignorance in not discovering before. Our much boasted modern science is like a child without a teacher—like a child in the dark, who finds something and wonders, till the light is brought and the new found thing proves to be some old coin or trinket that was worn before.

It is so with this study of the hands. Science on every side is bringing forward proof of its truth and of the mysterious principle of life with which it teems, the dust of centuries is being removed, facts are being dug up, and things are being spoken of in this century of surprises that go far to prove the truth of that old statement *that as the hands are the servants of the system, so all things that affect the system affect them.*

If people want facts in this age of materialism, they should remember that there is almost no study at the present time that can bring more facts to prove its authority than this study of Hindoo hermits and ancient seekers for a sign.

It is our system of reasoning, nowadays, to go back to the beginning of things, to trace the origin of the truth we have stumbled on in our delvings by the wayside ; therefore, in connection with this study the first fact we must face is its antiquity and its origin. There are many people who would be amazed, probably, to know that in antiquity it is older than Christianity itself ; that two thousand years before the birth of Christ it had its origin, and that away back in those regions where the snow-tipped Himalayas pierce the very heart of the heaven, this strange idea entered men's minds that the soul, somewhere and somehow, wrote out its own history—like the captive writing his name and legend upon the stones of his prison house, to be read or not as the case might be.

In the earliest language of the known world we find this idea expressed, and later on the lines and signs of the hand interpreted as the characters and language of the soul. We must remember that the people who gathered and fostered this science were famous for their study of mankind ; they studied men *as in our age we study machinery ;* and is it not probable that they brought their art to as much perfection as we have done with our wonders of electric cables, phonographs and so forth ? Where the first idea originated that the hand was the index of the mind, and consequently of the soul, will probably never be known, but it is sufficient for our purpose to find that in the Aryan civilization—the oldest in the world—this study was known and practised, and that since then it has had an almost unbroken record in that cradle of the Orient philosophy—the India of the East.

But, coming nearer home, we find that in the height of the Greek civilization this study found favour in the eyes of some of those ancient Grecian philosophers whose wisdom and knowledge has been the foundation of our modern schools of learning. When men like Anaxagoras, Aristotle, Paracelsus, Cardamus, Pliny, and Hispanus were found having the greatest belief and respect for this science of the hand, then people need certainly not be ashamed of also believing in it. It is only those who are ignorant of these facts who say that it is but " women and fools " who believe in palmistry, whereas we find that even Hispanus sent a book on this study to Alexander the Great, in which he wrote : " It is a study worthy the attention of an elevated and enquiring mind."

The reason that this old science fell into disgrace and into the hands of charlatans, tramps, and vagrants, can be very easily accounted for when one remembers that in the early ages it was indicted by the Church. As early as 315 A.D. the Ecclesiastical Court passed an edict punishing with excommunication, and even death, any person found practising palmistry " outside the Church." Can it be wondered at, then, considering such a law, and considering the power of the Church in those ages, that people were afraid to even say they believed, much less to practise it ?

During the centuries that followed, it was naturally loaded down with every kind of superstition, black magic, and " agency of the devil," but truth will always prove itself truth, by rising, phœnix-like, from the fires of persecution, and so it was in this remarkable case. In the year 1445, the same year that the Bible appeared for the first time printed with movable type, a monk, named Hartlieb, inaugurated a movement in favour of this study, and in 1474 he published a book on the subject, one of the first books printed with movable type after the Bible.

From this date there were many attempts made by intellectual people to have this study placed upon a proper basis. In England it was thought necessary to make laws against it, and so, following the rule laid down by the Church in the reign of Henry VIII., we find it classed with witchcraft, sorcery, etc., and the severest punishment framed against any person found practising palmistry.

Even as late as the reign of George IV. the Act of Parliament reads : "Any person found practising palmistry is hereby deemed a rogue and a vagabond, to be sentenced to one year's imprisonment, and to stand in the pillory."

In the nineteenth century, however, science came to the rescue of this so-called superstition ; the consensus of scientific opinion began to place the hand, as the immediate servant of the brain, under the direct influence of the mind, and the still more mysterious influence and subtlety of thought. Meissner, in 1853, proved the existence in the hand of the tactile corpuscles " running in straight rows in the red lines of the palm." He afterwards demonstrated that these corpuscles contained the ends of the important nerve fibres from the brain, and that during the life of the body they gave forth vibrations and crepitations, " distinct and different in every human being," *which changed under the influence of every change in the system*, and which ceased the moment life became extinct.

The late Sir Charles Bell, who was considered one of the greatest authorities of the present age on the nerve connection between the brain and the hand, commenced his famous Bridgewater treatise in 1833 by writing :—

" We ought to define the hand as belonging exclusively to man, *corresponding in its sensibility and motion to the endowment of his mind*."

The same scientist demonstrated in his work that

as there are more nerves from the brain to the hand than to any other portion of the system, that as the action of the mind affects the entire body, it therefore follows that every thought of the brain must more immediately affect the hand. The most pronounced sceptic will readily admit the great difference that exists in the hands of people of different temperaments. Nature does nothing without a purpose ; there must, therefore, be a meaning in such differences, as is the case with difference in animals showing peculiarities of breed and temperament. To the judge of horses, the slightest variation contains to his practised judgment a " language in a line." Why not in the observation of the hand ?

It also stands to reason that, if we can so easily prove that variation of shape contains a meaning, so then must every other variation in connection with it, whether it be of nerves, skin, lines, or nails.

Let us now turn our attention to the lines and examine the arguments both for and against.

The chief argument against this study is generally brought by people who, from ignorance or want of examination of cause and effect, rashly jump to the conclusion that the lines of the palm must be made by folding and constant use. This at first thought sounds plausible enough, but such an argument cannot, when considered calmly, hold ground.

In the first place, in medical work, it is a well-known fact that, in certain cases of paralysis, long before the attack takes place, the lines of the palm completely disappear, although the hand can continue to fold as before.

Again, and most important of all, if the lines were made by use, a woman working with her hands—say a seamstress, for example—and constantly folding them in her effort for daily bread, would, according to all laws of logic, have some thousands of lines and cross lines in her hands by the time she reached forty, while the woman of luxury and of ease would have scarcely any; but the direct opposite is the case, as can be proved by the most casual observation.

In my large work, "Cheiro's Language of the Hand," I have gone more deeply into the many arguments and scientific reasons for a belief in this study, and also in the examination of the question of destiny. I have not space at my disposal here to go more closely into this question. I must, however, for the sake of helping the student, should he have to undergo some cross-examination from some sceptical friend, bring forward a few reasons for the future marking itself on the hand in advance of the action.

In connection with this idea, it has been demonstrated by scientists that every portion of the brain may grow, diminish, or change, and correspond by such changes to those of habit, temperament, or talent used by the individual in the every-day actions of life. As the brain evolves from childhood to manhood, it follows that there must be an advance growth before it can reach its point of power or action. The slightest change, it will thus be seen, must affect the body in advance of the action, and, as before stated, that there are more nerves from the brain to the hand than to any other portion of the system, it is therefore not illogical to assume that the hand, to the student of such things, denotes the change going on in the brain, even years before the action of the individual becomes the result of such a change.

It has been proved that the lines in the hand have, like the nose, or the eyes in the face, a normal or natural position. The slightest deviation from the normal denotes abnormal qualities or tendencies, as, for example, the line of head falling to the wrist in the hand of a suicide, and rising and controlling the heart line (the better nature), as in the hand of a murderer. Therefore, if proved in one point that certain marks on the line of head show this or that peculiarity mentally, and that certain indications on the Line of Life are in relation to length of life or the reverse, the same course of observation, it will be seen, that can predict illness, madness, or death years in advance, will, if persisted in, be also accurate in its findings that marriage will occur at this or that point, with this or that result, and also in regard to prosperity or the reverse. Every other science has been built up by observation ; in this study of the hand the observations have been carried on through thousands and thousands of years. During my sojourn in India I was permitted to use and examine a book on the markings of hands, where the most accurate records had been kept of cases wherein lines, marks, and mounts were proven correct.

It must also be remembered that it is the accepted theory of scientific minds that, arguing from the standpoint of evolution, the brain of an individual at the age of twenty may commence a development of a talent or peculiarity that will alter the entire life at forty without the individual being conscious of any such change until, probably, the moment of action is reached, but, as that development in the brain causes a change in the brain nerves at twenty, so must it also cause a change in the entire nerve system, but, as shown earlier in the argument, more importantly in its effect upon the hand.*

Whether the influence that marks the hand be the "subtle essence of the brain," or a still deeper and more hidden power that "shapes our ends, rough hew them as we will," it matters little. Such agency or influence may for ever remain a mystery, but because it does, that does not qualify us for refusing to believe in it because we do not know. One might as well say, "I refuse to live because I do not know all that constitutes life," or, "I refuse to think because I do not know the processes of thought."

I have refrained here from touching on the question of fate, or the hereditary influences that fulfil the old law of "the sins of the fathers visited upon the children." I must, however, state that I consider the study of life teaches that men and women are born under *conditions that produce given results*, that the greatest pity should be extended the murderer, the suicide, or the unfortunate, and that it is only by the teaching of the Greek law of " Know Thyself " that humanity may be helped to rise out of

---

* It has been proved lately that grey matter similar to that of the brain can be found in the tips of the fingers of blind persons.

conditions that fetter it. That no church or sect or creed can emancipate with man-made laws and God-thwarted beliefs ; that nothing but the study of nature teaches nature ; that as God, nature and destiny are one, so by the knowledge of *our* destiny do we honour the Maker of it, to the fulfilment of His purpose, whether it seems good or ill to our finite understanding, for

> What does it matter at the end of life
> If we are victors crowned with spoil of strife,
> Or humbler soldiers in a well-fought fight,
> Who did their best—*and so their best was right ?*

CHEIRO.

CONTENTS

CONTENTS

PART I
CHEIROGNOMY

CHAPTER I

THE STUDY OF THE HAND

THE study of the hand is divided into two sections—the twin sciences of Cheirognomy and Cheiromancy. The first-mentioned deals with the shape of the hands and fingers, and the latter with the lines and markings of the palm.

As the limbs of animals differ in shape, contour, and proportion, and by doing so denote breeding, and hereditary peculiarities, so do the hands and fingers of individuals. As the judge of horses can tell from the shape of the limbs of the animal what one may expect through breeding, so may one be able to tell from peculiarities in the formation of the hands what the individual owes to the heredity of the chain of ancestors who have preceded him.

In the same way that a man would not expect the horse with slender, delicate limbs to do the work of the Clydesdale with its heavier development, so it is with hands ; the long-fingered, narrow hands have their own special department in life's workshop distinct and different from the short, thick-set class, and so on with every variety of the types. The study of the types is therefore a most interesting one, and one that can be more easily carried out than that of the study of the lines, as many people refuse to show the hand for an examination, whereas the type that the hand belongs to also indicates character and temperament with unfailing accuracy.

The difference in the shape between, for example, the French and the German, or French and English hands, would convince any thinking person that temperament is indicated largely by the shape of the hand, and although one might broaden and enlarge one's hand by work or certain kinds of exercise, yet it is a remarkable thing that the type remains the same.

There are seven types of hands corresponding in a measure to the seven races of mankind, and these again might be subdivided into seven varieties of the seven types, as I have clearly explained in my larger work.*

The seven types are :—

(1). The elementary, or the lowest type.
(2). The square, or the useful hand.
(3). The spatulate, or the active, nervous type
(4). The philosophic, or the knotty hand.
(5). The conic, or the artistic type.
(6). The psychic, or the idealistic hand.
(7). The mixed hand.

* "Language of the Hand," by Cheiro.

CHAPTER II

THE SEVEN TYPES OF HANDS

WE must commence to consider the seven types of hands by starting at the lowest, the Elementary, or, as it is often called, the Necessary Hand (Plate I., Fig. 1). This type indicates the very lowest type of mentality—it is on the border line between the brute and the man.

The hand itself is extremely short, thick-set and clumsy. The thumb also is unusually short, and barely reaches the base of the first finger : as a rule there are very few lines on such hands, seldom more than the three main lines, heart, head, and life.

People possessing such hands have little mental ability, they are found in occupations requiring only unskilled labour. Such people are very often extremely violent in temper, but not courageous ; they have little or no control over their passions, and are brutal and animal in their desires.

THE SQUARE HAND

The Square Hand (Plate I., Fig. 2) is so called because the palm is square at the wrist, square at :he base of the fingers, and with the fingers themselves square. This type is also called the useful, as it is found in so many vocations of the useful order.

The square hand is the most practical and logical of all the types; people with such hands are orderly and practical, more on account of their love of habit and custom than through their real sense of the fitness of things.

They are respecters of law and order in a nation, and are rather methodical in work, they have the greatest perseverance and tenacity of purpose, they weigh and measure things by rule and reason. They are usually sceptical of all things bordering on ideality, they want logic for belief, and are extremely stubborn in their convictions.

They have little originality or imagination, but in work they have such force of application, tenacity of purpose, and strength of their convictions, that they are usually successful.

They are sincere and true in promises—staunch in friendship, but not demonstrative in affection.

They make good lawyers, doctors, scientists, and business men, and their chief fault is, that they live so much by reason, that they lose the mystery of life in their search for the material.

THE SPATULATE HAND

The Spatulate Hand (Plate I., Fig. 3) is usually found crooked and irregular, with the tips of each finger something like the spatula chemists use in mortars.

This type can be found with the palm itself

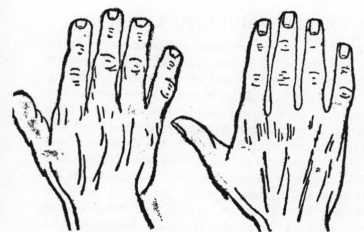

Fig. 1. The Elementary Hand.

Fig. 2. The Square, Useful Hand.

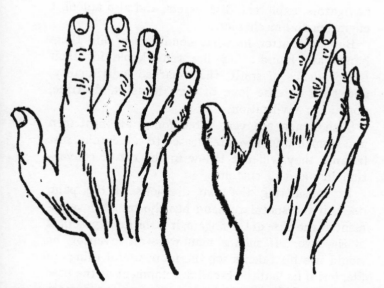

Fig. 3. The Spatulate Hand.

Fig. 4. The Philosophic Hand.

PLATE I.

spatulated, in two positions, either extremely broad at the base of the fingers and tapering back towards the wrist, or very broad at the wrist and sloping towards the base of the fingers. These two distinct characteristics we will take up and consider a little later. The spatulate hand may be either hard and firm, or soft and flabby. In the first-mentioned case it indicates a nature restless and excitable, but full of energy of purpose and enthusiasm ; if so, it is a magnificent type to possess, it indicates intense love of action, energy, and independence of spirit, a love of invention, discovery, and originality.

Such hands are largely found amongst great navigators, explorers, discoverers, and also amongst engineers and mechanics.

But no matter in what condition of life these hands are found, they are remarkable for their independence of spirit, their marked individuality, and their intense love of new ideas in doctrine, dogma, or civilization.

Such hands are very often found amongst men and women whom we are pleased to call cranks, just because they will not follow in the rut of conventionality and of custom.

In considering the two divisions of the palm itself, if the spatulate hand has the broad development at the base of the fingers, it is the more practical of the two. If such a man were an inventor, he would use his talents for the more useful things of life, but if he had the broad development at the base of the hand, he would be inventive in the domain of idealism, and his inventions would not take the form of useful or practical things.

If the spatulate hand is found soft and flabby, it denotes more a restless and irritable spirit ; such persons could stick to nothing long, they change with the mood of the moment, and are usually dissatisfied, discontented, and erratic.

THE PHILOSOPHIC HAND

The Philosophic Hand (Plate I., Fig. 4) is the most easily recognized of all. It is usually long and angular, with bony fingers and developed joints.

People possessing such hands have a marked personality distinct and different from individuals endowed with the other types. They are more or less peculiar in habits, actions, and ideas.

They are philosophers in some form or another, they seem to feel their marked personality, for though they are friendly to all, yet they have few close friends or associates. It is seldom that they gain great success in the form of wealth, and when they do, they use their wealth largely for others, they build houses for the destitute, schools for the poor, and are philanthropic in their thoughts even if they are peculiar in their views.

They are very often found as students of humanity, and often the greatest readers of character are found with people who have these philosophic hands. Such people love detail, neatness, and order, particularly in others ; one should be extremely careful of the details of dress if asking a favour from a man or woman with a philosophic hand.

In character they are silent and secretive, careful over little matters, even in the use of little words ; they are proud with the pride of being different from others, and they are often egotistical through that very belief in their own personality.

These people are always inclined to be religious, even if independent of any form of creed. The philosophic hands are largely found amongst preachers, poets, and writers. To be more accurate, I should say that they have a devotional sense more than a religious one, but if found in any excess of development they are then fanatical in religion and also in mysticism ; mystery in every sense appeals to them largely, and this might in fact go far to account for the mystical faith that forces them to be devotional rather than religious.

In considering these hands it must be borne in mind that the developed joints are the peculiar characteristic of the thoughtful and the philosophic, while the smooth pointed fingers are the reverse. As well, the development of the joints gives the love of analyzing, but it must be remembered that it is the shape of the hand and also the position of the Line of Head which decide whether the power of analysis be used for chemicals, or for mankind.

The tips of the fingers on a philosophic hand may be either pointed, square, or spatulate, as the case may be. In such cases the action and ideas of the individual will be largely influenced by the peculiarities of the square, conic, or spatulate temperament.

THE CONIC HAND

The Conic or Artistic Hand (Plate II., Fig. 1) has very often misled people on account of its name ; people seeing it often simply called the artistic hand have been carried away by the idea that the man who paints pictures, or the musician, must necessarily have this type of hand. On the contrary, this type simply indicates the love of art and of the beautiful in every shape and form. People with such hands rarely carry out their artistic ideas. The reason for this may be found in the fact that people with this type have not one quarter the continuity of purpose of people possessing a more square or more philosophic formation.

The conic hand has in fact often been called the " hand of impulse." Those with such hands as a rule do not wait to think or use their judgment, they act on the impulse of the moment—they show an artistic, impulsive nature, in which the love of luxury and indolence usually predominate.

Such people, though they may be quick and clever in thought and ideas, tire so easily that they rarely carry out their designs or intentions.

They are, however, excellent conversationalists, they grasp the drift of a subject quickly, but it must be confessed that they are more or less superficial; they can learn quickly almost anything, but they have not the power of the deep student through want of application.

Such people are rather easily offended over little things, they are also impressionable to the people they come in contact with and to their surroundings.

Women with such hands love admiration even more than is the custom of their sex, they are also very susceptible to affairs of the heart ; they cannot live without love, but they are children of moods, and they must love very deeply before one can be very certain of the constancy of their affection.

People with this type of hand like or dislike at first sight, and carry such feelings to extremes ; they are also quick-tempered, but temper with them is but a thing of the moment.

When out of temper they are brusque, and speak their mind too plainly for their own good, and are too impetuous to study words or expressions.

They are generous and sympathetic, to a certain extent selfish when their own personal comfort is concerned, but their love-nature is so strong that their sympathies rule in the end.

It is a much better sign to find this type of hand firm and elastic, than full and flabby. In the latter case such people are selfish, they consider their own personal comfort first, and everything will be sacrificed to their love of luxury and indolence.

THE PSYCHIC HAND

The Psychic Hand (Plate II., Fig. 2) is the most beautiful but the most unfortunate type of all to possess, that is if we consider worldly advancement. The pure type is, however, very hard to find, as our modern civilization does not encourage the

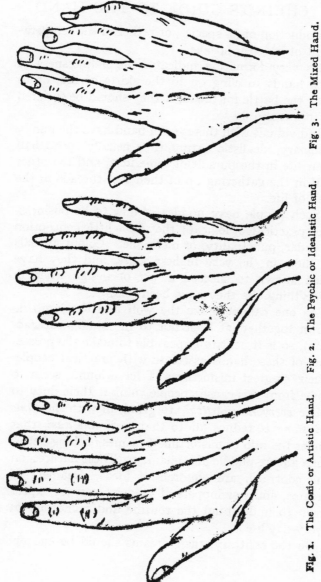

Fig. 1. The Conic or Artistic Hand.   Fig. 2. The Psychic or Idealistic Hand.   Fig. 3. The Mixed Hand.

PLATE II.

reproduction of its species, or rather of the temperament of which it speaks.

Its very formation indicates the helplessness of such hands to cling on to the skirts of life, or to fight the battle for bread, if they should be so fated as to have to do so.

Individuals with this type of hand have the purely visionary, idealistic nature, they usually spend half their life in the pursuit of some idea, and the other half in the gathering up of their lost threads in the web of life.

Such people have no idea of how to be business-like, practical, or logical ; they have little conception of order, punctuality, or discipline. Colour appeals to them in the very highest sense, and they have been known to succeed in art or design when in everything else they have been failures.

As one cannot make the wolf and the lamb lie down together (at least not to the lamb's satisfaction), so is it next to impossible to make the possessors of these hands associate with practical people. Their greatest misfortunes, I have found, seem to come from this cause ; people think it their duty to *make everyone practical*, to grind all with the *same millstone*, to reduce all to that *same fine dust*, that under the rain of misfortune becomes nothing better than a mere puddle of humanity.   These natures, on the contrary, are children of ideas, dreamers of dreams, and worshippers of visions ; can we expect them to understand the routine and monotony of every-day life ?

On the contrary, their dreams should be encouraged, their idols restored, and their ideas fostered. Does the lily grow by being placed in the desert ? Does the hot-house flower thrive if we expose it to the frost ? It is the same way with humanity : we are tones and semitones in life's great harp ; there is the treble and the bass, the major and the minor, all are necessary to life's grand harmony; let them be then, *all that is—is best.*

Individuals possessing the psychic hands are very often extreme fanatics in religion and orthodox creeds, or else they use their devotional spirit in mysticism, and become devotees to fanciful ideas of occultism, and usually go to an extreme either one way or the other : the Line of Head, which will be explained later, may give them a balance that they would otherwise not have, but that is a point outside the consideration of the meaning of the type of hand.

THE MIXED HAND

This last type is the most difficult of all to describe, it is so called because not only the fingers, but the hand itself, cannot possibly be classed under a head such as square, spatulated, etc. (Plate II., Fig. 3).

It is as if all the types have taken a part in the building up of this seventh. For example, the first finger might be found pointed, the second square, the third spatulated and so on. When such is the case it denotes an individual full of versatility, but as changeable in purpose as the sands of the sea. Such a man would be adaptable to all sorts and conditions of ideas or circumstances, but erratic and uncertain in the use of his talents. A man with such a hand might play a little, paint a little, sing a little, and so on, but rarely, if ever, will he be great. If a strong head line ruled the hand, there would then be a chance of his succeeding in some one thing that he would like best and so force himself to stick to; but as this is so rarely found, the mixed hand is generally put down as belonging to a talented dilettante who will never stick to anything long enough to succeed.

NOTE

The student should remember that through the breedings and intermingling of races the pure or exact type is rarely found. Hands are more often found as containing two or three types together, as the palm might be square while the fingers might be pointed or philosophic, or there might be three types together, as, for example, the palm square, the fingers, near the hands and second joints, philosophic, and the tips pointed or spatulated. If this is borne in mind it will assist greatly in forming a more accurate opinion of the subject's character, and getting at certain points in the disposition that would otherwise be concealed or unexplained.

CHAPTER III

THUMBS: THEIR DIFFERENCES AND PECULIARITIES

IN the judgment of character, the thumb is almost of the same importance to the hand that the nose is to the face (Plate III.). It expresses more especially the strength or weakness of the natural will of the individual, and is one of the most significant indicators of character in connection with this study. The thumb has also played a prominent part in the various civilizations of the world, as shown by customs both civil and religious that hold their own even to the present day.*

Looking at this study from a scientific standpoint, the thumb alone would go far to prove the remarkable nerve connection between the brain and the hand. It is a well-known fact to all nerve specialists that there is what is known as a " thumb centre " in the brain, and that if there is any undue pressure on this portion of the brain, a certain form of paralysis is bound to be the result, and furthermore a certain peculiarity of growth takes

---

* In the " Language of the Hand," I have explained at length the various points of interest in connection with the thumb as regards customs, religions, and so forth.

place in the nail phalange of this important member of the hand, and is an actual and reliable warning of disease even years before it becomes manifest in any other portion of the system. And yet, in the face of this fact, which has long been fully demonstrated, there are hundreds of medical practitioners who consider it " looks wise " to pooh-pooh a sensible and scientific study of hands, for fear it would bring them even on the confines of that much abused study called palmistry.

However, the medical profession is becoming more broad-minded as centuries roll by. The ever-increasing light of knowledge has dispelled many of the old prejudices ; hypnotism, that fifty years ago was rejected as even more absurd than palmistry, is to-day recognized and taught in their colleges. It is similar with this study of the hand ; certain shapes have been proved to go with certain diseases, the nails are also studied, and during the autumn of 1895 in Boston, U.S.A., I had the honour of having in one of my classes five of the leading physicians of that city.

THE TWO DISTINCT CLASSES OF THUMBS

There are two distinct classes into which the study of the thumb may be divided, namely, the firm jointed one and the supple. It must be first borne in mind that the strength or weakness of the will as shown by the thumb may be modified by the Line of Head, which shows the development or non-development of the individual. The simplest rule to follow is, that the shape of the hand and fingers denotes the inherited disposition, the development of the lines denotes the acquired, whether through cultivation or environment. The thumb, it will thus be seen, indicates the temperament of the parent from whom the child inherits most, and although other differences of character might come in to make certain changes in after development, yet if the thumb of the child is, say for example, supple jointed like the father's, the *natural* will of the child will be found to be exactly similar to the natural inherited will of the father.

The rules to be observed are as follows :

The firm jointed thumb (Plate III., Fig. 2), denotes a more obstinate will and determination than that of the bendable, supple jointed kind ; it is as if the firm jointed thumbs are more made to resist, and if their lives were carefully watched, it would be found that they have to resist and fight their way more in life than people possessing the other class. When the firm jointed thumb is large and full in the nail phalange, it then gives obstinacy of character rather than determination of purpose.

The supple jointed thumb (Plate III., Fig. 3) on the contrary denotes a more pliant nature, yielding readily to surrounding influences, unless the Line of Head is found unusually straight. In such a case the individual would have a *developed mental will* and determination that would in many ways offset the inherited pliant nature. This trait of pliancy rarely, however, goes with such strength of will and determination as that found with the firm jointed thumbs.

The supple joint may either be found to the nail phalange of the thumb or to the joint of the second phalange, this difference makes an enormous distinction in itself. In the first place the nail phalange supple jointed denotes a nature extremely adaptable to people ; the second phalange supple or double jointed denotes the nature adaptable to *circumstances.* Individuals with the supple jointed thumb (first phalange) are less strict in their views and ideas than those possessing the firm jointed type, it also goes with great generosity, extravagance, and often prodigality. It must be remembered, however, that such generosity may often result from the very trait of adaptability to people which this class of thumb denotes. One will find people with such a class of thumb more easily swindled and more ready to quixotically part with money than those of the firm thumb. A man with the latter-mentioned thumb might be just as generous at heart, but more practical in the carrying out of his liberality ; he would be less easily imposed upon, and would be less impulsive in all his dealings with money matters.

Another most important point to observe is the angle made by the position of the thumb to the hand.

There are two very simple rules to follow in connection with this, namely :—

The more obtuse the angle made by the thumb, the more independence of will, and action, and generosity will be noticed in the life ; nothing must, however, *go beyond the normal* even in this case. If the thumb lie off the hand, as it were, or stand even

Fig. 1. The Clubbed Thumb.

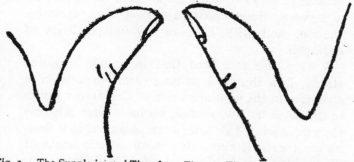

Fig. 3. The Supple-jointed Thumb.   Fig. 2. The Firm-jointed Thumb.

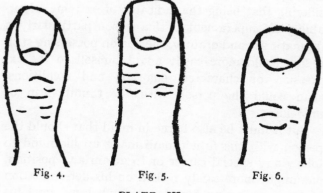

Fig. 4.   Fig. 5.   Fig. 6.

PLATE III.

at right angles to the palm, it denotes too much independence of will and obstinacy for the owner's own good. Such individuals will be almost impossible to control or manage, they will always be more or less in trouble and continually in a state of insubordination to rules, regulations, or laws

The thumb the opposite of this, namely, lying so close as to make an acute angle to the hand, denotes a nervous, timid spirit, a person with excessive caution, and with little or no independence of character.

I have also remarked that in occupations, the strong, firm thumb finds its greatest expression of character in the administration of the sterner duties of life, such as law, science, business, etc., whereas the supple jointed denotes a temperament that finds its most natural expression in all artistic walks of life, and has especially a greater field in dramatic art, oratory, etc., and this might be explained by considering that being the indicator of extreme adaptability of temperament for that reason, particularly in dramatic art and oratory, the person possessing such a sign could more easily adapt himself to the expression of character, emotion, and conditions, than could the person with the thumb firm or unyielding.

But it must be also borne in mind that should the person with the firm thumb make up his mind to follow any special career or to attain any position, one might more safely reckon on his determination of purpose forcing him to gain whatever goal his ambition might lead to.

THE THREE SECTIONS OF THE THUMB

The thumb proper in this study of the hand is divided into three sections called the phalanges of—

1. *Love.*

2. *Logic.*

3. *Will.*

Number 1. Love (Mount of Venus, Frontis.), is that portion of the thumb upon which the Mount of Venus is situated.

This phalange, as it is called, if long, indicates strength and power of emotion in matters of affection, but if with it Venus is high or very fully developed, it gives sensuality to the nature.

If short and thick set, with Venus full, the subject would be the victim of his passion and emotional temperament. The phalanges, No. 2 and No. 3 (*see* Frontis.), should be more or less equally balanced ; if No. 2, the phalange of Logic, is extremely long, then Logic and Reason over-master the force of Will, and the result would be indecision as to the execution of plans, extreme deliberation, and uncertainty of action.

On the other side, No. 3, the phalange of Will, should in its turn not be so long as to over-master No. 2. In such a case it would denote unreasoning Will, a nature always in opposition and consequently in conflict with others.

The third phalange should on the contrary be well made, neither too short nor too long ; it should also not be too pointed nor yet too square at the tip.

The following rules may help the student in the study of this most important member of the hand :—

1st. A long thumb, well proportioned, denotes the subject's inheritance from a long line of intellectual antecedents.

2nd. A short, thick-set, brutish looking thumb, the reverse (Fig. 6, Plate III.).

3rd. A very pointed thumb denotes an erratic will, impetuous and uncertain (Fig. 4, Plate III.).

4th. A square thumb, thick at the end, an obstinate, self-willed person (Fig. 5, Plate III.).

5th. A hollow waisted thumb (Fig. 4, Plate III.) want of logic, but a person gifted with tact and diplomacy.

6th. No. 2 phalange (Fig. 5, Plate III.) thick and clumsy at joint, want of tact.

7th. No. 3 phalange extremely thin—want of force of will.

8th. No. 3 phalange extremely thick—a brutal, overbearing will, obstinate and aggressive (Fig. 6, Plate III.).

9th. No. 3 phalange with what is called the Clubbed Thumb* (Fig. 1, Plate III.) a sign of ungovernable temper, a brutal, aggressive nature, a lack of reason in action, blind, unrestrained passion aroused by the slightest opposition.

Such a thumb is largely found among those who commit murder in a moment of passion, and also amongst persons who have lost all control of their temper, and is generally accompanied by a craving for stimulants of all kinds.

---

* Considering that, as I have shown earlier in this chapter (*see* p. 15), there is a distinct Thumb Centre in the brain, and that specialists in nerve diseases are well able to tell by twitchings, peculiarities in the shape, etc., that a certain form of paralysis is threatened through a pressure on this part of the brain, it is, therefore, not illogical to assume that the particular growth called the "Clubbed Thumb" (Fig. 1.) is the visible sign of some such pressure, which, instead of producing paralysis of the body, produces that ungovernable violence of passion which is a disease in itself—or, as physicians delight to call it, "*an unbalanced state of the mind*"

CHAPTER IV

OF THE DIFFERENT SHAPES OF FINGERS AND THEIR SIGNIFICATIONS

THE Ancient Hindus conceived the poetical idea that "the gods dwelt in the tips of the fingers." Long before the modern idea of "the laying on of hands," "relief by the hands," etc., the electric magnetism of the fingers had been described in pictures and statues dedicated to Hindu worship. It has taken nearly nineteen hundred years of our wonderful modern civilization (?) to prove as true the so-called theories of the past. Among the many supposedly visionary ideas, the one that stands out more clearly than all the rest is that strange truth of "the virtue of the fingers" that the ancient Hindus voiced in their poetical idea that the tips of the fingers were the habitations of the gods.

In the statues and images of this wonderful people, the position of the hands, and more especially of the fingers, had in every case a special meaning.

If the thumb were uppermost, or if concealed, if the first two fingers were raised or depressed, thus was the dumb image of god, idol, or demon carved to converse in silence with some greater power to which even in stone they still appealed.

Modern science has proved that the tips of the fingers are, for the greater part, the termini of the brain nerves. The passive or active mind is therefore in direct communication with the finger tips, and as we all possess certain qualities that *live in us*—qualities of gods or demons, as the case may be—it follows that this ancient race in their figurative and poetical expressions were not so far off from actual facts as many of our modern " Wise " have at times attempted to make out.

The importance of this idea can easily be seen when one considers that every finger has in some way a distinct individuality of its own, and ought, therefore, to be closely observed and noted if one wishes to treat this subject with sincerity and from a scientific standpoint.

When the hand is thrown open and falls into its own natural position, it may be that the first finger, or the third, or even the fourth assumes a position which is so full of character that it cannot fail to be observed. It was to this point that the Greeks paid marked attention, and it was owing to this that they gave to each finger its particular name, as indicative of the attributes of various gods in their own mythology. (*See* Map of the Hand, Frontis.).

The first finger is called the Finger of Jupiter.

The second   ,,   ,,   ,,   Saturn.

The third   ,,   ,,   ,,   The Sun
                                              or Apollo.

The fourth   ,,   ,,   ,,   Mercury.

A little study of Greek mythology will show that the gods of the Greeks were simply a representation in form and fable of man's ambitions, passions, virtues, and vices. Therefore, when one takes the hand and places it in a natural position (palm upward), the finger which appears as the dominant finger will be found to give a decided keynote to the entire character.

The following table shows the qualities indicated by the different fingers, which of course vary slightly according to the power expressed by the finger itself.

THE FINGER OF JUPITER

Long.	*In excess.*
Love of power.	Tyrannical.
Command over people.	Extreme egotism.
Power to rule.	

Short.	*Crooked.*
Non-aggressive.	Lack of principle in rule
Dislike of responsibility.	and ambition.

THE FINGER OF SATURN

Long.	*In excess.*
Prudence.	Morbid desires.
Love of solitude.	

Short.	*Crooked.*
Frivolity (especially if pointed).	Morbid sensitiveness.

THE FINGER OF THE SUN

Long.	*In excess.*
Love and worship of art.	Desire for speculation.
Desire for celebrity.	Craving for notoriety.

Short.	*Crooked.*
Dislike to publicity.	Lack of principle in their
Less love of art.	desire for notoriety.

THE FINGER OF MERCURY

Long.	*In excess.*
Mental power. Influence with people. Power of expression, especially in speech.	Extreme diplomacy. A desire to cover actions by deceptive language, etc.

Short.	*Crooked.*
Slow in grasp of ideas. Easily foiled in plans.	Lack of expression, easily influenced by people.

The fingers should be long in proportion to the palm. It is well to bear in mind that the growth of the fingers represents the distinction between " ideas and materialism." Atheists generally have large palms and short fingers. People with long fingers, on the contrary, will quickly accept ideas, and very long hands and fingers often belong to individuals who are extremely visionary and fanciful.

Long fingers give love of detail in everything, but though they analyse they may not be one atom logical. Lawyers, for example, generally have short fingers and a square hand. Long fingers worry and fidget over little things more than the short fingers ; they are often inclined to curiosity, and will never rest if they think they have only been told " half a truth."

Short fingers, on the contrary, take things more *en masse*, they are also more impulsive, quick in thought and action, and, if the fingers are square, extremely logical.

Fingers set evenly on a straight line, or nearly so, across the top of the palm are often found on most successful people's hands. They indicate great evenness of temperament and a well-balanced nature. This point has not received the attention that it merits, but I have found it possesses the very greatest significance.

Another important point is to consider if the fingers have dropped, as it were, into the palm.

If, for example, Jupiter is out of line and set low on the palm it reduces the power of command over people, and is often found with a nature that is awkward and uneasy with strangers or in society and extremely sensitive in coming in contact with people. Jupiter set high would give the reverse.

Saturn is seldom set out of its place.

The finger of the Sun dropped low into the palm gives a nature that will find the recognition of the world hard to gain, at least as far as celebrity or art is concerned.

The finger of Mercury low would tell against the subject in business and financial matters ; his temperament would not allow him to " use " people for personal interests, and he, on the contrary, would always be open to being swindled and easily influenced in matters of finance.

THE LEANING OF THE FINGERS TOWARDS ONE ANOTHER

If, when the hand lies open, all the fingers lean out towards the first, it denotes an ambitious spirit, independence of character, and an aggressive nature that is inclined to fight its way forward.

If Jupiter turns towards Saturn, the reverse spirit is indicated, and there is more melancholy in the nature.

If all the fingers lean towards Saturn then extreme sadness and melancholy may be expected, and even a rather morbid desire of being different from others.

Saturn towards Jupiter gives rather morbid ambition.

Saturn towards the Sun denotes vast contradictions in the nature. A person greatly swayed by moods : one moment bright and joyous, the next despondent.

The finger of the Sun leaning towards Saturn often denotes the desire for notoriety in some morbid sense.

The Sun leaning towards Mercury gives a combination of art and business, generally the artistic sense sacrificed to the value of money; whereas Mercury leaning towards the Sun would give business sacrificed to art—the practical qualities, for example, that one finds associated with business

D

or science turned in the direction of art. A hand with all the fingers straight and well developed is, however, more powerful and successful than any of these combinations.

The first finger standing very much to itself and sticking outward denotes a most ambitious nature and desire to command.

THE SPACES BETWEEN THE FINGERS

A wide space between the thumb and first finger indicates generosity of nature, broad-minded qualities, and independence of will.

Between Jupiter and Saturn—independence of thought.

Between Saturn and the Sun—independence of circumstances.

Between the Sun and Mercury—independence of action.

If the fingers appear loose and are rather supple and separated, it shows unconventionality and dislike to restraint. If, on the contrary, they all lie tied down together it denotes conventionality, fear of custom, and of " what people might say."

Fingers supple jointed and curved backwards show quickness of mind, they grasp facts and people easily, are adaptable in nature, but more or less swayed by the mood of the moment.

Fingers stiff and curved inwards—slowness of mind ; such people do not easily grasp ideas and are generally self-contained, rather timid, and in a measure more wrapped up in their own ideas, and are usually very sensitive.

THE PHALANGES OF THE FINGERS

The three phalanges of the fingers represent the three great worlds of thought :

Ideality, Reason, and Materiality

The first or nail phalange long, gives the love of ideality in all things.

The second phalange, if large, the love of reason.

The third phalange, if long, the love of material things.

If the third phalange is full and thickset, it indicates a love of the good things of the table, luxury, ease, and comfort. If, on the contrary, this phalange is small or waist-shaped at the base, the subject cares little for the table, and can easily do without luxury and appears not to miss it in any sense.

CHAPTER V

THE NAILS

ONE of the most interesting sections of the study of the hand is that of the nails (Plate V.). Almost a volume in itself could be written on this side of the subject alone, for the nails not only indicate temperament, but they are also remarkably sure guides as to hereditary tendencies towards disease.

Medical men in London, Paris, and America have lately taken up this study of the nails with great interest; during my visit to Boston in 1895, five of the leading physicians of that city attended my classes, and I hold some remarkable testimonies from them as to the practical value they obtained from a study of the nails alone. Space will only allow me in this book to give in as concise a manner as possible the leading qualities and diseases indicated.

The nails are divided into four distinct classes, namely, long, short, broad, and narrow.

Long nails are seldom found with great physical strength; they threaten delicacy to chest and lungs (Plate V.), and when much curved both from the

top back towards the finger and across the finger,
the danger is more accentuated.

There is still greater delicacy of the constitution
indicated when these extremely long nails are deeply
fluted and ribbed.

Even if the subjects themselves do not actually
suffer from the lungs or chest, a little examination
will disclose the fact that such a tendency has been
in the family, and no matter how strong the individuals appear to be, they ought to be warned that
care must be taken in all matters relating to pneu-
monia, colds, etc., etc.

The same type of nail, only shorter and generally
broader, indicates a tendency in the system for
throat trouble, such as inflamed throat, laryngitis,
asthma, catarrh, and bronchial affections (Plate V.).

Long nails, wide at the top and very bluish at the
base, denote bad circulation and weak action of the
heart. Nails not showing any moons, whether long
or short, denote weakness of the heart, and indicate,
even years in advance, a tendency for heart failure.
On the contrary, the moons very large, above the
normal size, indicate excessive forces of circulation,
rapid action of the heart, etc.; the subject in such
cases should be warned against over excitement and
all stimulants. In such cases there are usually two
points in the system threatened:

1st. A breakdown of the valves of the heart.

2nd, Great rushes of blood to the head—
tendency to apoplexy.

It is very easy to find out which of these two
diseases is likely to prevail: namely, if the Line of

Head runs on to the Mount of Mars (*a-a*-Plate VI.), the head will be affected, and this is all the more certain if the Line of Head shows any signs of islands (*a—a*—Plate VII.).

If, on the contrary, the Health Line is the most pronounced, running from the Line of Heart into the Line of Life (*j—j*—Plate VI.), then the chief danger will be the heart, and unless care is taken the result will be valvular heart disease.

SHORT NAILS

Short nails (Plate V.) without moons run in whole families where there is a tendency for bad circulation and weak action of the heart. The worst form is when they are thin and flat at the base, with no moons. Short nails, very flat and sunken into the flesh, show nerve diseases and a tendency for paralysis. Short nails, very flat, shell-shaped (Plate V.), and inclined to lift or curve out at the edges, are sure signs of paralysis, and particularly so if the base of the nail is bluish in colour.

People with short nails have a greater tendency to suffer from heart trouble and from diseases affecting the trunk and lower half of the body.

Long nailed people, on the contrary, are more liable to trouble in the upper half of the system, namely, lungs, chest, throat, and head.

Narrow nails, long, threaten weakness of the back and if extremely narrow, high, and much curved, spinal trouble (Plate V.). Thin nails, very small, denote delicate health and want of vitality.

White spots all over the nails show an over-

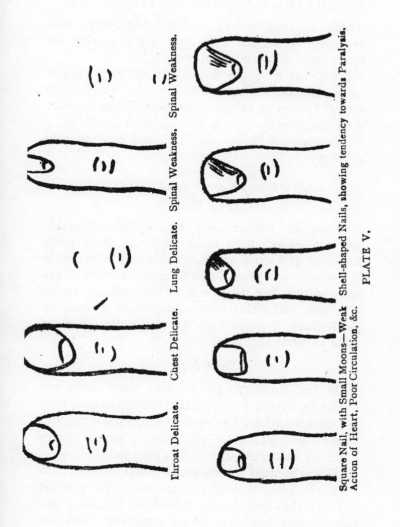

Throat Delicate. Chest Delicate. Lung Delicate. Spinal Weakness. Spinal Weakness.

Square Nail, with Small Moons—Weak Shell-shaped Nails, showing tendency towards Paralysis. Action of Heart, Poor Circulation, &c.

PLATE V.

strung, nervous system, and on thin hands with very faintly marked lines they are generally the forerunners of nervous prostration.

When the nails are fluted, the entire system is more delicate ; when, however, the fluted nails appear broken by corrugations going in the opposite direction, namely, across the nail, such breaks show arrested growth in the nail itself and consequently delicacy.

DISPOSITION AS SHOWN BY THE NAILS

Long Nails.

As regards temperament, long-nailed individuals are less critical than those with the short nails. They are also more impressionable and more gentle in temper ; as a general rule their owners take things more easily, but they are rather inclined to be visionary, and shrink from looking facts in the face, particularly if those facts are distasteful to their ideas of what should be.

Short Nails.

On the contrary, people with short nails are extremely critical, even of things relating to self; they are more sceptical, they analyse thoughts, ideas, and actions, and incline to logic, reason, and are more practical than individuals with long nails.

When the nails are naturally much broader than they are long, it indicates rather a quarrelsome nature ; they love debate, opposition, etc., they will take almost any side of an argument, and are extremely obstinate and hard to convince.

Nails, short by the habit of biting, indicate a nervous, highly strung temperament ; in such cases the nervous system is more or less impaired.

White spots on the nails denote that the system is run down through nervous strain or worry. The spots, however, only appear after the strain or illness. They are often found in cases where a person has had a sudden demand upon his nervous force, for example, to appear before the public, or to be called upon to fill some responsible position, or some great strain of anxiety. All undue demand upon the nervous force will cause, with some temperaments, the appearance of these spots, but when the nails are covered with them all over, it is a sign that the nervous system has run down, and generally through nervous worry and anxiety.

NOTE

I do not pay any attention to the old superstition of white spots or black dots on the nails having any other meaning but that in connection with health, as explained above.

CHAPTER VI

THE MOUNTS OF THE HANDS AND THEIR MEANINGS

IN my system I class the Mounts with Cheirognomy or the study of the hand, independent of the lines. The Mounts indicate the constitutional or hereditary qualities, the same as the shape of the hands denotes racial peculiarities, breeding, and so forth. I must also state at this point that manual labour will not depress or increase these Mounts, although, of course, labour will have the effect of coating them with a heavier cuticle; still the natural position and shape of the Mount will remain the same.

I might also here explain that in the use of the old-time names, such as Mounts of Venus, Mars, etc., they are not used by me in any superstitious sense whatever. Even the Greeks, who gave such names to different portions of the hand, did so as a kind of mental shorthand way of describing qualities by the use of names. For example, it has been observed that some people have what are known as Venus qualities, namely, the desire for love, for admiration, etc., and this has been more noticed in those individuals who possess the Mount at the base of the thumb high, so naturally it became in time known as the Mount of Venus; and so on, with every other Mount, the names have been given to illustrate characteristics. If people will only bear this in mind, this study will at once assume a more logical and scientific character, and will be more in accordance with the grave study of humanity to which this much abused study of hands has been a long lost key.

THE MOUNT OF VENUS

The Mount of Venus (Frontis.) is that development or non-development, as the case may be, found at the base of the thumb. This Mount, it should be remembered, covers one of the largest and most important blood vessels in the hand—the great palmar arch. Looking at the question, even from this standpoint, it follows that when this mount is large, there is a greater flow of blood through this arch, consequently we may expect to find greater robustness of health and consequently a more passionate nature, with all those qualities relegated to Venus—that much abused Goddess of beauty and love. When not abnormally large, this is one of the most favourable Mounts on the hand. It indicates a warm, sympathetic, and lovable nature—a desire to please, to be admired, to be loved. People with this mount well marked have always considerable desire for luxury; they have great taste in colour. music, and art. They are impressionable to surroundings and to people; they are warm-hearted, generous, and usually impulsive.

In excess, like everything else in life that is abnormal, it is usually ruinous in the end. In either sex the desire for admiration is, in such a case, the weak point, and coupled with that we find a sensual temperament. The desire for luxury and self-indulgence exaggerated, and so on with every point that in the normal is beneficial, in the abnormal is as equally ruinous as the first-mentioned is favourable.

THE MOUNT OF JUPITER

The Mount of this name is found at the base of the first finger (Frontis.). When well developed it denotes ambition, pride, enthusiasm in anything attempted, a desire for power, and generally the love of control over people, principle, honour, and love of justice. In excess, over-weening ambition, egotism, a tyrannical love of power and a dictator in every sense of the term

THE MOUNT OF SATURN

This is found at the base of the second finger (Frontis.). It denotes love of solitude, quietness, prudence, earnestness in work, a desire for the study of sombre things, such as psychological questions, occult philosophies, and generally an appreciation of music of the classical and sacred order.

In excess—extreme melancholy, sensitiveness to people, great depression of spirits, and morbidness.

THE MOUNT OF THE SUN

This Mount is found at the base of the third finger and is also called the Mount of Apollo (Frontis.).

When well developed, it indicates a love of all things beautiful, whether one follows an artistic career or not. It gives a love of painting, poetry, literature, sculpture, and all imaginative work appealing to the emotions through the mind.

In excess, the Mount of the Sun, as its very name would imply, would denote love of glory, publicity, notoriety, and show.

THE MOUNT OF MERCURY

The Mount of Mercury (Frontis.) has a peculiar significance of its own. Like the planet Mercury in astrology, it leans to either good or bad ; on an evil hand this mount, large, makes the evil worse, on a favourable hand, it is most auspicious. It denotes all the mercurial qualities of life—love of change, travel, excitement, wit, quickness of thought and power of expression, but with a straight head line success in science or business is denoted.

NOTE

If the finger belonging to any mount is very long, the effect will be similar to the mount being itself well developed.

For example, the first finger (Jupiter) long—the desire to rule, to dictate, to have authority, etc. ; people with this finger short, as a rule, dislike the responsibility of office or of position.

THE MOUNT OF MARS

There are two Mounts of Mars; the first is found beneath the Mount of Jupiter, but inside the life line, and above the Mount of Venus (Frontis.). This, the first, gives active courage, great presence of mind in danger, and usually the desire for a martial life. In excess, it denotes a quarrelsome, fighting, and aggressive spirit.

The second Mount of Mars is found between the Mount of Mercury and that of Luna (Frontis.). It denotes passive courage, self-control, resignation, in fact—moral courage as opposed to physical courage, indicated by Mars number one.

THE MOUNT OF LUNA

This Mount lies on the side of the hand below the second Mars and directly opposite Venus (Frontis.). It indicates refinement of thought, imagination, love of beauty, more in nature than in people, love of scenery, romance, ideality, imaginative literature, generally poetry. In excess, there are few Mounts more dangerous, the imagination becomes too great, they become visionary idealists, the children of theories, and the worshippers of ideas ; the romance is overshadowed by vain sentiment, and unless the head line is extremely good, this Mount in excess is one of the most dangerous signs. Luna and Venus, close together and large, are, as a rule, associated with a sensual, voluptuous, and luxurious nature, where the senses and the passions, as it were, go hand in hand.

THE LEANING OF THE MOUNTS TOWARDS ONE ANOTHER

When the Mounts lean towards one another, the qualities of each are blended together. For example, if Saturn leans towards Jupiter, it gives the latter some of its love of sombre things, its prudence, its melancholy, and its religious tendency ; the ambitions of Jupiter would consequently be also in keeping with the qualities of Saturn ; and so on with every other Mount.

CHAPTER VII

THE PALM, AND LARGE AND SMALL HANDS

A VERY thin, hard, dry palm indicates timidity and a nervous, worrying, troubled nature. A large, soft palm shows a phlegmatic and indolent disposition.

A thick, heavy, coarse palm, very soft, shows sensuality and general coarseness.

A hollow palm has been proven to be a most unfortunate indication ; I have also noticed and proved a peculiarity not mentioned by any other writer on the subject, namely, that the hollow may incline more to one line or portion of the hand than to another ; the following rules I have therefore observed.

If it inclines to the Line of Life, it indicates disappointment and trouble in domestic affairs, and if the rest of the hand denotes ill-health, it is a further sign of delicacy and trouble.

When the hollow comes under the Line of Fate, it strongly suggests misfortune in business, money and worldly affairs.

When under the Line of Heart it tells of disappointment in the closest affections.

A firm, elastic palm is a sign of energy, of enthusiasm, and of active will.

A soft, flabby hand is the reverse : it denotes indolence, want of firmness of purpose, and a phlegmatic nature.

LARGE AND SMALL HANDS

It is a very strange fact that, speaking generally, people with large hands do very fine work and love detail in work, while those with very small hands go in for big ideas and cannot bear detail in employment.

Small hands, as a rule, organize and go in for plans often completely beyond their power of execution ; even the writing of small hands is often remarked to be large and bold.

E

PART II
CHEIROMANCY

CHAPTER VIII

A FEW REMARKS IN REFERENCE TO THE STUDY

BEFORE we go farther, there are one or two points I would like to place before the attention of the student. In the first place, I will not pretend, as so many do, that it is a simple thing to master this study by just fixing a few rules in one's head, or reading a book through and then throwing it aside. On the contrary, if one considers the subject at all, one will be struck, not only with its importance, but with the intellectual care and thought that must have been expended on it by the ancient Hindus and Greek philosophers, and others who, in our own day, have tried to clear it from the rubbish and superstition of the middle centuries.

We know how difficult all study is, but how much more so is the study of life itself, with its phantasies of mind, and brain, and soul, not to speak of the network of surroundings, " influences " and hidden laws that play their part in the grand machinery of evolution and of destiny. The one fundamental thing necessary in this special study is conscientious work, patience, and perseverance, but the reward—ah, the reward is equal to the labour. To be able to read the hand is to be able to read the secret book of nature, that volume whose pages are human lives, whose covers are Life and Death, and whose clasp is that golden thread of hope that runs through all men's hearts.

If this is borne in mind, the student will be satisfied to proceed slowly and surely : he must remember that as there are no two natures alike, *so there are no two hands alike,* and that, as with every person, something new must be expected, so he cannot expect to succeed by blindly using set rules without always combining with those rules a severe exercise of his own mentality.

The next point to be borne in mind is the difference of opinion which will be met with and which is often used by thoughtless people as an argument against this study. On the contrary, we should remember that difference of opinion exists in all phases of thought ; where, might I ask, can such difference be better illustrated than, for example, amongst doctors and scientists of all descriptions ?

As regards my own work, I shall be found to differ from other writers in a great many instances. The only claim I make for my system is that it has been formulated after years of study, research and *practical professional experience,* and that there is not a rule given either in this book, or in my " Language of the Hand," that has not first been demonstrated in hundreds of cases.

One of the principal points of difference in my teachings and those of others is, that I class the various lines under different heads, dealing with each particular point.

I contend that this will be found, not only less puzzling, but also more in accordance with reason. For example, I hold that the Line of Life relates to all that affects life, to the conditions and influences under which it exists, to the length of life from all natural and hereditary causes.

I regard the Line of Head as related to all that affects the mentality, and so on with every other line, as will be seen later. This plan I hold to be more in accordance with logic and science than systems that set out to tell a broken heart from, probably, a mark on the head line, or an accident to the head from the life line, and so forth ; besides, I claim for my system that it enables the student to translate the new lines that he may meet and which may not be explained in any book, but if he works from this system it will enable him to class the new line or mark, and consequently to find out its meaning.

CHAPTER IX

THE LINES OF THE HAND

THERE are seven important or main lines on the hand and seven lesser lines. The important lines are as follows :—

The Line of Life, which embraces the Mount of Venus (Frontis.).

The Line of Head which is found crossing the centre of the palm (Frontis.).

The Line of Heart, which runs parallel to that of the head at the base of the fingers (Frontis.).

The Girdle of Venus, found above the Line of Heart and generally encircling the Mounts of Saturn and the Sun (Frontis.).

The Line of Health, which runs from the Mount of Mercury down the hand (Frontis.).

The Line of Sun (Frontis.), the line found ascending to the third finger.

The Line of Fate, which ascends the centre of the hand to the Mount of Saturn (Frontis.).

THE SEVEN LESSER LINES

The Line of Mars, which rises on the Mount of Mars and lies within the Line of Life (Frontis.).

The Via Lasciva, which is found parallel to the Line of Health, as it is in its worst form, viz., running into the Mount of Venus (Frontis.).

The Line of Intuition, which extends like a semi-circle from Mercury to Luna (Frontis.).

The Line of Marriage, the horizontal line on the Mount of Mercury (Frontis.), and

The Three Bracelets, found on the wrist (Frontis.).

The Main Lines are known by other names as follows :—

The Line of Life is also called the Vital.

The Line of Head, the Natural or Cerebral.

The Line of Heart, the Mensal.

The Line of Fate, the Line of Destiny, or the Saturnian.

The Line of Sun, the Line of Brilliancy, Line of Fortune, or Line of Apollo.

The Line of Health, the Hepatica, or the Liver Line.

A useful thing to remember is that the hand is divided as it were into two parts or hemispheres by the Line of Head.

The upper part, comprising the fingers and Mounts of Jupiter, Saturn, the Sun, Mercury, and Mars, represents Mind ; the lower, comprising the base of the hand, represents the Material. This division has hitherto been ignored, but it is almost infallible in its accuracy, as, for example, when the predisposition is toward crime the Line of Head rises upward on the right hand and crushes the heart line, and as well increases the size of the lower part of the palm.

CHAPTER X

L INES should be clear and well marked, neither broad nor pale in colour; they should be free from breaks, islands, or irregularities of any kind.

Lines pale in colour indicate lack of robust health, and in temperament, lack of energy and decision.

Lines red in colour denote an active, robust temperament, they also show a sanguine, hopeful disposition.

Yellow lines, as well as being indicative of a bilious temperament, also denote a nature self-contained, reserved, proud, in contradistinction to the qualities shown by the red lines.

Lines extremely dark in colour tell of a melancholy, sombre temperament; they are generally found with natures self-contained, revengeful, and unforgiving.

Lines *may* appear, diminish, or fade, a point which must always be borne in mind when reading the hand. The province of the student of this science is therefore to warn the subject of approaching danger, by pointing out the evil tendencies of his nature or constitution. I hold that we largely make our own fate by our temperament—of course *we did not make ourselves*, so here we are brought back again to hereditary laws, " the sins of our fathers," and various other causes, over which we have little or no control. In answer to the question, Can people save themselves or avert an evil threatened ? I say yes ; also that character building is possible ; but in the same breath I add, that they rarely, if ever, do ; some who inherit strong will, do, I believe, in many cases, but they are the exception, and as a student of this work can very easily see how the subject has or has not averted certain evils in the past, so can he also, from the same grounds, be very well able to reckon whether or not portended evils in the future are likely to be changed, or frustrated.

The main lines change very little, and not at all in some cases ; if the two hands have remained the same, then there is less likelihood of any change in the future, particularly if the subject has passed twenty-one years of age.

A single evil sign must, however, never be accepted as decisive. If the evil is important almost every principal line will show its effect (and it is only logical that such should be so), and both hands must be consulted before the final decision should be given; the *tendency* is often shown on the left hand, whereas the fulfilment is denoted by the right.

When an important line, such as that of head or life, is found with what is called a sister line, namely, a fine line running by its side, it denotes that the main line is strengthened, bridged over for example by this mark, and the danger is lessened, if not altogether prevented.

Forked lines, when they are main lines (a forked line of head, for example), give greater mental power, but they also denote more or less of the " double nature."

A chained formation is a bad sign in any line : on the line of heart it denotes weakness and change-ability of affections ; on the line of head, want of fixity of ideas ; and on the life line it shows weak-ness of vitality.

Breaks in any line denote its failure.

A wavy formation weakens the power of any line ; it denotes instability of purpose in connection with whatever the line indicates.

A network or multitude of little lines, running aimlessly in all directions, betrays mental worry, a highly nervous temperament, and generally a troubled nature.

(These points are further illustrated in dealing with the main lines following.)

CHAPTER XI

THE LINE OF LIFE

What we know as life is but existence,
A waiting place, a haven by the sea:
A little space amid immeasured distance:
A glimpse, a vista, of that life to be.
                                          CHEIRO.

IT is an admitted medical fact that in every person born into this world there lurks the germ of disease, or tendency that may, one day, prove fatal. If such, then, is the case, the germ of disease may be known to the brain years before it has become sufficiently developed to commence its ravages upon the body, and, consequently, it is only reasonable to assume that, through the action of the brain upon the hand, it may be marked on that part of the body long before the stethoscope or other mechanical appliances can discover it.

The great difficulty in teaching people to understand the meaning of what is called the Line of Life lies in the fact that the majority of people start off with the preconceived idea that a long line going round the base of Mount of Venus (Frontis.) must necessarily mean that the subject will have a long life. In the main idea this is correct ; if the line is *perfect*, without breaks, crosses, or irregularities of any kind, it does promise that such a life should be healthy and extremely long ; but how very seldom is this found—in my experience only in one case to every hundred.

But most important of all—the Line of Health (Frontis.) must be considered, if one is to attempt to judge accurately of the length of life. I will treat of this line separately a little farther on ; but in connection with the Life Line, it must be borne in mind that if these two lines should at any place meet, *if one line be equal to the other*, then the age indicated by that place of meeting will be the period of death.

If even the Line of Health be extremely deeply marked at any place, and the Line of Life is weakly marked, or there is any island on it *opposite* the deeply marked Health Line, at the age thus indicated death is likely to take place, although, to the casual observer, the Life Line looks as if it goes round the base of Venus.

Another sign that threatens ill-health, and sometimes even life itself, is when a heavy line falls, as it were, from the Mount of Saturn and goes through or even touches the Line of Life (*c-c*-Plate VI.). This has never been considered in any modern works on the subject, although it is alluded to in some of the older MSS. ; it is a mark that has interested me deeply for some years, and I have always found it particularly accurate, and on many occasions saw that it accounted for illness and sometimes death, being exact to the year, and the only bad mark or

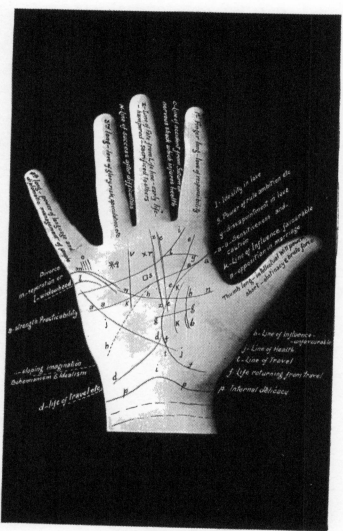

PLATE VI.

fantastic sign on an otherwise good hand (for dates and calculations of time see Plate IX.). The above points cannot be too closely watched if the student desires to be accurate as to predictions of illness and threatened death. One of the great advantages of the study lies in such warnings—it is only *when people are ill that they go to the physician*, whereas the illness might have been averted, or at least modified, had they known what tendencies towards diseases they had either inherited or by habits were predisposed to.

The Line of Life is that line which rises under the Mount of Jupiter and running down the hand encircles the Mount of Venus (Frontis.). It not only relates to illness, death, and the constitution of the subject, but the events of other important lines are often verified by it.

This line should be long, narrow, and deep, without irregularities or breaks of any kind. Such a formation promises length of life, good health, and vitality.

When the line is made up of little pieces like a chain (*b—b*—Plate VII.), or found splitting into little hair lines, it is then a sure sign of bad health, and particularly so if this is found on a soft hand. When the line recovers its evenness and continuity, health and vitality are regained.

The two hands must always be consulted in considering marks of illness and death; when broken on the left and joined on the right, it generally means some dangerous illness at the point where the break occurs—but if absolutely broken clean off in both hands—death. This is all the more certain when one branch turns back on the Mount of Venus (*a*—*a*—Plate VIII.).

When the line starts sloping downward from the Mount of Jupiter, instead of starting at the side of the hand, it denotes an ambitious life from the commencement.

When the line is connected with that of the head without the two lines clinging very much into the palm, it is a good sign, denoting caution, carefulness, and, as a rule, continuity of purpose ; such people are, however, very sensitive, and generally lack sufficient self-confidence.

When these lines are extremely interwoven together, the subjects are retarded by super-sensitiveness, they are too easily crushed and discouraged in the struggle for existence. This detrimental and unfortunate quality could be greatly altered if parents would notice this early in life and endeavour by training to change the nature before the little one goes out into the battle alone.

A medium space between these two main lines is an excellent sign (for further remarks on this, see chapter on Line of Head)—it denotes that the subject is more free to carry out the plans of the life ; such people are also ambitious and have great energy, self-confidence, and a go-ahead spirit (*b*—*b*—Plate VIII.).

When the Line of Life divides above the centre of the palm, and one branch shoots across to the base of the Mount of Luna (*d*—*d*—Plate VI.), it indicates, on a firm hand, a love of change, travel,

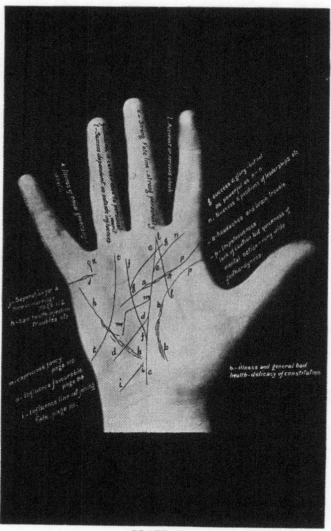

PLATE VII.

and the ultimate satisfaction of that desire ; on a flabby, soft hand, however, it always denotes a restless nature craving for excitement, but if with a sloping line of head, the love of excitement will be gratified in stimulants or intemperance of some kind, in such a case the flabbiness of the hand shows an indolent nature, too lazy to travel or undergo fatigue.

A crowd of little hair lines dropping from, or clinging to the Line of Life tells of weakness and loss of vitality wherever they appear ; these are distinguished from lines of travel that start from the same line by the fact that these little hair lines are found *on the inside* and *outside of the Line of Life.*

Lines of travel, which generally involve some great change of place, climate or country, are found as fine lines leaving the Line of Life, going out through the plain of Mars and generally ending on the Mount of Luna.

All lines that rise upward from the Line of Life towards the Mount of Jupiter are marks of increased power, gains, and successes. If one of these lines ascend far up into the hand and end on or to-wards the base of the first finger, it denotes some great increase of power—generally some position of authority over others—for the first finger is the dictator or finger of authority—the lawgiver of the hand (*e—e*—Plate VI.). Lines may rise from the Line of Life and terminate on the other Mounts of the hand, as well as that of Jupiter. To read such lines the rule to follow is that such a mark takes after the particular Mount that influences it and on which the line ends.

A line rising from the Life Line, for example, and finishing on the Mount of Saturn, is similar to a Fate Line which has been concealed or tied down by the Life Line for years ; if there is no Fate Line in the centre of the palm, this latter mark becomes, therefore, all the more important, and from where it starts ought to be read as a Line of Fate or Destiny ; if, however, there is a Line of Fate on the hand as well, it then reads of something attempted by the subject which is different from his regular career, and which will run parallel with his career (z—z—Plate VI.).

To distinguish between lines that rise from the Life Line to Saturn (which are advantageous), and lines that descend from Saturn to the Life Line (which are unfavourable), the following rule must be closely observed, viz. :—the line rising from the Life Line is much heavier or thicker at its starting place than where it finishes, and *vice versâ*, the line from Saturn is much heavier where it starts from than where it finishes on the Life Line ; this is considered by some a very troublesome point, but surely a rule like the above makes it not only simple but logical.

A line from the Life to the Mount of the Sun indicates glory and success due to the subject's own life, and not to outside circumstances or to chance.

To Mercury (this must not be confounded with the Line of Health), it denotes some special success, generally in business or science, but again, like the other indications, whether they be to Jupiter, Saturn, or the Sun, success through the person's own life and effort.

When the Line of Life divides towards the end and the outside branch (towards the percussion) is longer and more important than the other, it denotes that the subject will travel greatly and will end his life in some place or country away from the point of birth.

If the inner line, on the contrary, is the more powerful, no matter where the persons travel to, or what lands they live in, they will always return again to the land of birth, if not exactly the place of birth (f—f—Plate VI.).

An island on the Line of Life denotes illness or loss of health as long as the mark lasts—but a large, clear island at the very commencement of the Line indicates, according to most authorities, some mystery in connection with the subject's birth. I have noticed that in many cases this is correct, but it is so hard to get information on this point, that such a rule can hardly be said to be definitely established.

The Line of Mars (Frontis.), found inside the Line of Life, must not be confounded with attendant lines which are found springing off or out of the Line of Life itself. The Line of Mars rises on the Mount of Mars, and follows in some few instances the entire course of the Life Line, or may fade off about the centre, as the case may be.

The Line of Mars on all broad, square or spatulate hands, gives excess of health, rather a fighting disposition, and is an excellent sign on a soldier's hand, as it gives courage, love of danger, etc.

On a narrow, thin hand, it supports even the most delicate Life Line, helping it, as it were, by its excess of vitality over breaks, islands, or all marks of ill-health. It, however, generally goes with irritability of temperament ; such people are more than usually in hot water with their neighbours.

When a heavy branch line shoots out from this Line of Mars to the base of Luna, it is also often the sign of intemperance, particularly so if the Head Line also rises high on Mars number two.

Influence lines are those fine lines that lie inside the Line of Life. They denote friendships, generally with the subject's opposite sex, and by the length and duration one may tell how long such an influence has lasted ; a man or woman with what is known as " the Venus temperament " will have these lines much clearer and more full of detail than natures who are not so much ruled by their passions and emotions.

I have not space at my disposal to go into all the details of such lines here, but if people wish to study them farther, they will find in my large work full information about such marks and their meanings.

Lines running in the opposite direction, viz. :— cutting the Line of Life (g—g—Plate VI.), show worries and obstacles caused by the interferences of others—those marked early on the Life Line are generally caused by relatives, those lower down are more often oppositions by people in the ordinary affairs of life. An excellent rule to follow is that the lines running parallel with the Life Line are influences of one's opposite sex—those crossing it, one's own sex.

If one of these "opposition lines" cut or interfere with the Line of Fate it is much more important, as it denotes that at the date *it touches the Fate Line* some person will interfere with the career.

When such a line touches the Sun Line, the interference will be to one's fame, good name, or position.

To the Line of Head, great brain worry and anxiety.

To the Line of Heart, interference with one's closest affection.

To the Line of Marriage, interference with one's marriage, and so on with every line or point of the hand on which such a line ends.

Many lines on the Mount of Venus running parallel to the Line of Life denote a nature very dependent upon affection ; such persons have many love affairs and attachments in life, in fact they crave for affection, and are never happy unless they feel that people love them. The same Mount without any lines, denotes a nature less influenced by such things, they are more indifferent as to whether they are liked or not.

Many lines crossing in the opposite direction, viz. :—outward, denote that such a person allows people dangerous to their interests to come too much into their life ; such persons are continually in trouble through the interferences caused by those they come in contact with.

Very few lines coming outward, on the contrary, denote the nature that keeps to itself, that does not allow people to mix much with its plans or projects, and consequently such an individual has less trouble and interferences in going through life.

As regards time, the calculation of events, and the division of the Life Line, the student will find a special chapter devoted to this point farther on in this work

CHAPTER XII

THE LINE OF HEAD

" To know is power "—let us then be wise,
  And use our brains with every good intent,
That at the end we come with tired eyes,
  And give to Nature more than what she lent.
                                        CHEIRO.

THE Line of Head (Frontis.) relates to the mentality of the subject, to the intellectual development, and to all illness and diseases that may affect the brain.

The Line of Head may rise from three distinct points, viz., from the Mount of Jupiter, the Line of Life, or from the Mount of Mars inside the Life Line.

Rising from Jupiter, but slightly touching the Line of Life, it is, if a long line, probably the most powerful of all (a—a—Plate VI.). Such a subject would have great brain power, determination of purpose, ambition, and power of control over people, coupled with logic, reason, and sound judgment. Such persons are excellent in positions of responsibility and authority, and in the administration of justice to others.

There is a variation of this class which is almost

equally good. This again rises on Jupiter, but keeps slightly separated from the Line of Life ; this gives less caution than the first mentioned, but is also excellent for the management of people and plans. People possessing such a mark rise to every emergency of life ; their greatest fault is they are inclined to lack continuity of purpose, they are impetuous, impatient, and cannot brook the control of others (b—b—Plate VIII.).

If, however, this space is very wide, the subjects will then be rash, imprudent, and rather foolhardy in the way in which they dash into things without thought ; this is even still more the case on a woman's hand.

The Line of Head from the commencement of the Line of Life and joined with it is a well-balanced, favourable sign, provided there is a good Line of Head, viz., one long and clear. Such people are very cautious, generally too much so for their own advantage, they are also extremely sensitive, and have little self-confidence ; this is the direct opposite sign from the Head Line with the wide space of Jupiter. If the two lines, Head and Life, be still more tightly joined together, and travel like this far down into the hand, the super-sensitiveness of such a nature will greatly interfere with success in life.

The Line of Head rising inside the Life Line on the Mount of Mars is not a favourable sign—it indicates a fretful, worrying nature, one always in quarrels and conflict ; it is also an extremely nervous, sensitive sign, which may largely account for the irritability of such persons.

The leading points indicated by the Line of Head are as follows :—When straight, clear, and even, it denotes practical common sense and a love for material things more than the imaginative—when straight in the first half, then slightly sloping, it shows a balance between the purely logical and the purely imaginative; such a person will be very level-headed, even when dealing with imaginative ideas.

When the entire line has a long, gentle slope, the general tendencies are imaginative, it denotes love of art, literature, music, and such like.

When very sloping on the Mount of Luna, it denotes intense idealism, imagination, love of the romantic and Bohemianism (*h—h*—Plate VI.). This is all the more intensified when found on such hands as the philosophic, conic, and psychic ; on these types it is a most dangerous sign if it goes very much to the wrist or base of Luna, the imagination of idealism generally runs completely away with such people, such subjects very often commit suicide, which has given rise to the idea that it must always mean suicide, but people do not take into consideration that it must be taken with the type of hand on which it is found ; on a square type, for example, it would not be half so dangerous as if found on the conic or psychic, for the reason that the shape of the square hand in itself indicates practical common sense and materialism, so that the shape would act as a kind of balance to the imaginative qualities of the mind : it always, however, goes with a melancholy tendency and an excess of imagination, and when found on a narrow, psychic hand, with other signs unfortunate, it foretells the tendency towards suicide.

The direct opposite of this would be the Head Line *rising upwards*, and so crushing the love nature (the Line of Heart), but this must not be confounded with one straight line across the palm, which, as it were, is a combination of both head and heart, but unless the Line of Destiny is good, this is not a fortunate sign to possess.

In the first instance, one must remember that the Line of Head should be, more or less, normal in its position across the hand ; anything out of the normal must be abnormal in either one direction or the other, as the Head Line sloping gives the tendencies for imagination, ideality, and everything, in fact, the opposite of the practical nature —money getting, etc., so the line rising gives the development of the absolutely practical, the love of money and the harder nature (*a—a*—Plate VI.).

One main line across the palm of the hand is a sign not found in more than one to the hundred. It either promises great success or great failure ; if the Fate Line be shown, then it is generally great success ; if no Fate or Sun lines, I have generally found it to mean failure. It is a combination of both Head and Heart joined together. It shows great intensity of feeling in all cases where the palm is firm. if such persons put their mind to anything they carry it out against all reasoning and all opposition ; if they place their heart or their affections on any one it is done in the same way. They are rarely understood, and feel themselves greatly alone in life ; they either show extreme indifference to success, or extreme desire for it ; there seems to be no medium to such natures, but one single redeeming line on such a hand would alter everything in their favour, as for example, a good Line of Fate ; such a sign with men produces magnificent soldiers or sailors—in action or danger the intensity of such an individual would carry them through any crisis. I have known personally two or three cases of soldier-heroes whose hands have had this very unusual mark.

A long, clearly cut Line of Head is a sure sign of good intellect and brain power.

A very short line, the reverse—dull intellect, and no quickness of intelligence.

When wavy and uncertain, it denotes an erratic, unstable quality.

When marked by little islands, great pain to the head, and generally poor memory (a—a—Plate VII.).

When broken in two pieces under the Mount of Saturn, it threatens death through some accident to the head ; an island under Saturn is also a sign of accident or injury.

When the line is so high on the palm that it leaves a very narrow space between it and the Line of Heart, it denotes that the head will always rule the heart.

If a branch from the Line of Head rises upwards and joins the heart, it indicates that some great fascination or affection will rule the subject's life. in which he will become blind to reason and danger,

A double Line of Head is rarely found, but if found, is a sign of brain power, but of some curious kind. Such people have, as it were, a perfectly dual mentality, one side (if one line be joined to the Life Line) gentle and sensitive, the other ambitious, determined, and self-confident.

They have great versatility, command of language, and a power of seeing almost every side of a subject ; their greatest fault, as far as success lies, is in the fact that they are intensely critical, and pull self and self's ideas to pieces as much as they do other people's. Such marks are as seldom found, and are as odd in their class, as that of the one straight line across the hand.

The Line of Head rising or sending branches up, or on to the Mount of Jupiter, is a sign of a very ambitious nature, and if the Head Line is good, it promises great success in the desires of such a person (c—c—Plate VIII.).

Above all it must be remembered that the Line of Head must be studied in connection with the type or class to which the hand belongs ; for instance, the sloping Head Line is more usual and more in accordance with the conic type, consequently a straight Head Line found on such a type would indicate a more strange development of the practical mentality (due to training or circumstances) than such a straight line on a square hand. The student should, therefore, keep the peculiarities of the various types well in mind when studying the Line of Head.

CHAPTER XIII

THE LINE OF HEART

*   *   *   *   * Keep still, my heart,
Nor ask for peace, when care may suit thee best,
Nor ask for life, nor joy, nor even rest,
But be content to love, whate'er betide,
And may be, love will bring thee to Love's side.

CHEIRO.

THE Line of Heart (Frontis.), otherwise called the Mensal, may rise from three important positions, viz. :—the middle of the Mount of Jupiter, between the first and the second fingers, or from the Mount of Saturn.

Rising from the centre of Jupiter, it gives the highest type of love—the pride and worship of the heart's ideal. A woman with such a mark must, above all things, be proud of the man she marries ; she would seldom marry beneath her, for the man of her choice must be great—one that she could look up to, if possible ; he must have position over other men (*i—i*—Plate VI.).

Such a woman would, however, be very easily wounded in her affection—through her pride—and once her ideal was broken it would be broken for ever, at least as far as that person was concerned.

The farther the Line of Heart goes up through

Jupiter to the base of the finger, the more jealous the natures will be in their affections, they are more exigent, and are very much inclined to dictate and rule the person they are in love with. If the line is abnormally long, going from side to side right across the hand, the more intense the subjects are, and the more likelihood of their being jealous when they do love.

The Heart Line rising from *between* the first and the second fingers, is the most favourable sign on the hands of man or woman ; this sign goes with a calmer temperament in matters of the heart, they are less demonstrative than those enthusiasts with the line from Jupiter, but they are very deep and strong in their devotion—if they love they forgive all faults, forget all failings ; though their idol fall a thousand times, they will calmly restore it in their hearts, they will even patch the broken feet of clay and go on again as before. This mark is more found on the hands of women than on men.

The third main position for the Line of Heart is from the Mount of Saturn. This denotes a more sensual quality in connection with the affection. It is often found that such a line from Saturn has very few branches or deviations : it simply consists of a heavy deep red line sweeping through the palm. People with such a mark are generally selfish in their affections, very sensual and voluptuous. The more the line rises from the finger itself, the worse they are in such matters.

The Line of Heart marked by a crowd of little lines continually running into it denotes inconstancy, flirtations, a series of *amourettes*, but no lasting affection.

When the Line of Heart is bright red, it shows great violence and intensity of the passionate temperament.

When pale and broad, the person is *blasé* and indifferent.

When very thin, like a thread, and pale in colour, the subject is cold, with little passion or affection.

When marked full of islands, the affections will be filled with sorrows and misfortunes.

When found close to the Line of Head, the heart will always interfere with the affairs of the head.

When, on the contrary, the Line of Heart is very high on the hand, with the Head Line rising also very close to it, the head will completely rule the affections, and a very practical nature in such matters is the result.

Breaks in the Line of Heart tell of disappointment in the affections.

The Line of Heart, forked and rising on the Mount of Jupiter, is a sign of trueness of heart in man or woman.

The Line of Heart rising on Jupiter (*i—i*—Plate VI.) is a sign of a happier disposition in matters of the affections. The line dropping downwards denotes unhappiness, and such people have more disappointments in their affections than fall to the lot of most mortals.

A most unfortunate sign is that of the Heart Line itself dropping downwards into the Line of Head (*d—d*—Plate VIII.), it indicates disappointments in one's affections.

The Line of Heart very bare, thin towards the percussion, is generally understood to show sterility, at all events it can be proved to mean that as the person advances in years, so do they lose all their power of affection.

If the Line of Heart has, as it were, faded out either altogether or in certain places, it is an ominous sign of such terrible disappointments in affections, that the person has finally lost all desire for the love of others, or feelings of emotions. There are, however, very few cases of this kind, for love is so closely woven with life, that we can scarce lose one without losing the other.

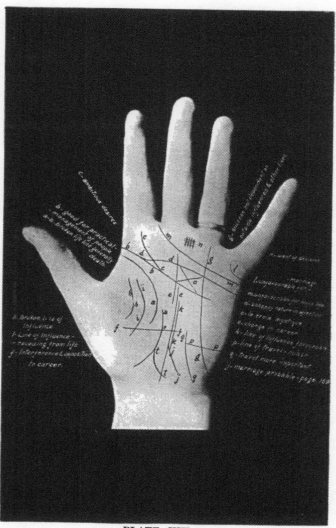

PLATE VIII.

CHAPTER XIV

THE LINE OF FATE

And would we question Fate ? Methinks
In life's long chain we are the little links
That stretch the endless whole ; and thus I teach :
As part of life—so are we part of each.

CHEIRO.

THE Line of Fate (Frontis.), also called the Line of Destiny, or the Saturnian, is one of the most important lines in connection with this study.*

In considering this line, the type of hand on which it is found plays a most important part ; for example, this line even in the most successful cases will be found less marked on the three first classes, viz.:—the elementary, the square, and the spatulate, than on the philosophic, the conic, or the psychic. This upright line is, as it were, more in keeping with the latter mentioned types and more found on them, therefore

* From the Indian Drama, written in Sanskrit, of Sakurstalá of Kalidas, 1st century, B.C.

Priest : Soothsayers have predicted that your first born will have universal dominion. " Now, if the hermit's daughter bring forth a son with the discus or mark of empire in the lines of his right hand, you must admit her immediately into your royal apartments with great rejoicings ; if not, then determine to send her back as soon as possible to her father."

King : " I bow to the decision of my spiritual adviser."

if one sees, as one often will, an apparently very strong Line of Fate on a conic or psychic hand, it cannot be taken to have the same importance as an equally strong line on the square, spatulate, or philosophic. This point has been completely overlooked by other writers on the subject, and the result is most puzzling to the student, as he may see what, in comparison, may seem to be a very slight, poor line of destiny on a square or spatulate, and come to the conclusion that it has very little meaning, and at the same time he may go into raptures over some upright line in the conic hand.

The Line of Fate, properly speaking, relates to all worldly affairs, to success, failure, to barriers, obstacles, against one's purpose in life, and to the people who influence our career. This line may rise from the wrist, the Line of Life, the Mount of Luna, the centre of the palm, or even from the Line of Heart.

Rising from the Line of Life, success will be won solely on one's personal merits, but if rising close to the wrist and is then drawn in or tied down, as it were, by the Line of Life, it denotes that one has sacrificed at least the early part of one's career to home influences, family ties, or such like affections, that have prevented success in one's early years. When such is seen the date where the Fate Line leaves the Line of Life has been the important commencement of success.

When the Line of Fate commences at the wrist and goes straight and clear to its termination on Saturn, it denotes a strong personality and is generally a good sign to have, for, in spite of all obstacles, such individuals always seem to succeed (*c—c—* Plate VII.).

From the Mount of Luna success is far more changeable and uncertain and always rather dependent on the fancy or caprice of others. This is very often found on the hands of public favourites.

A straight Line of Fate with an equally strong branch running into it from Luna (*d—d*—Plate VII.), is somewhat similar ; it denotes the influence of some person who would have a great deal to say as to the success of such a career, but again all these lines of influence from Luna usually denote changeable or capricious people who influence our career.

On a woman's hand these lines are usually found more deeply marked than on the hands of men.

If this influence line is deep and more powerful-looking than the Line of Fate, and afterwards runs on parallel to it, it denotes a wealthy influence or union, and is generally found tallying with the date of marriage (*see* Marriage Indications, Chapter XVII.).

If the Line of Fate sends off-shoots or lines towards any other Mount but that of Saturn, it denotes that the qualities of that particular Mount will dominate the life.

If the Line of Fate itself should go to any Mount other than that of Saturn, it promises unusual success in the qualities of that Mount, as, for example, if it sends a direct branch or goes itself to Jupiter (*n—n*—Plate VII.), it promises exceptional distinction and power—generally the power of the dictator over people ; such individuals have enormous energy, ambition, and determination in carrying out their plans, and they are especially good in government of people and in positions of the most serious responsibility.

If the Line of Fate terminate by crossing its own Mount and going to that of Jupiter, success will be so great towards the end of the career, that it will go far towards satisfying the ambition of even such a subject.

When the Line of Fate goes over the palm and runs into the finger of Saturn itself, it denotes that everything goes too far with such a subject. They have success, it is true, but things always seem to go beyond their control.

When the line is abruptly stopped by the Line of Head, it denotes that one destroys his career by some blunder of the head, and if the line does not go on farther it shows the loss is irreparable.

When the same thing happens at the Line of Heart, it signifies that the career is ruined through the affections.

The Line of Fate not rising till the middle of the hand—the plain of Mars—signifies a hard and difficult life, but if from that out it goes on well, the subject will surmount all difficulties and succeed in the end.

It is similar if it rises only from the Line of Head—it promises success from middle life, but through the subject's intellect and brain power only.

Rising from the Line of Heart, success will come

extremely late in life (about fifty), but life up to that would be nothing but a hard fight.

The Line of Fate with one branch from Luna, the other from Venus, denotes that one's career will always sway between imagination and love or passion.

When broken or made up of little pieces, the career will be very uncertain, with great ups and downs of success and failure.

Any decided break in the line is a sure sign of misfortune or loss, but if one line commence before the other leaves off, it signifies a complete change in life, and if the line looks favourable afterwards it is usually a change for the better and in accordance with the subject's own desires and wishes (e—e—Plate VIII.).

A double or sister Fate Line is often a good sign if they stand out clear and distinct in the palm, but if one runs from Venus, the other from Luna, it means a kind of strange, double life, very eventful, and not one to be desired.

A double Fate Line is, however, a good sign if they run side by side and go to different mounts ; it denotes a double career, two destinies successfully carried out if the lines are favourable.

All lines crossing the Line of Fate denote persons who interfere with one's career ; the date of such interference is given where the lines cut or cross the Line of Fate (f—f—Plate VIII.).

The Line of Fate is the most important line on which to consider dates (*See* Chapter XXII.)

CHAPTER XV

THE LINE OF SUN

And there are some who have success in wealth,
And some in war, and some again in peace,
And some who, gaining their success in health,
See other things decrease.
Man can't have all—the sun consumes itself
By burning in its lap more feeble stars,
And those who crave the Hindu idol's part,
Oft crush their children 'neath their gilded cars.
CHEIRO.

THE Line of Sun (Frontis.), otherwise called the line of brilliancy, the line of Apollo, or the line of fortune, like the Line of Fate, must be considered with the type of hand on which it is found; the same rule, therefore, which applies to the Line of Fate applies to this.

I prefer in my work to call this mark the Line of Sun, as it is less confusing. This mark increases the success promised by a good Line of Fate; it also makes the life more full of brightness, glory, celebrity, and position. If, however, it is not in accordance with the other lines of the hand, viz. : if there were little or no Fate Line, or a very bad Head Line, it then denotes only a nature longing for such things often a person with a keen appreciation of art, without, however, any power of expression. With even ordinary good lines, however, the Line of Sun is always favourable, in fact, in nine cases out of ten it may be assumed that, whenever it rises on the hand, that from that date things are going to improve and be more successful for the subject.

The Line of Sun may rise from the Line of Life, the Mount of Luna, the Plain of Mars, the Line of Head, or from the Line of Heart. Rising from the Line of Life, with the rest of the hand artistic, it is one of the best signs for success in some artistic career, but it is also, in this position especially, one of the greatest indicators of a sensitive temperament ; such persons would devote their entire life to the worship of the beautiful, and yet not make as much out of their lives as people with the Line of Sun from the Fate Line itself.

Rising from the Line of Fate it increases whatever success is promised by that line. In most cases it means distinction of some kind from whatever date it leaves the Line of Fate; it naturally follows that the clearer and the better the line, the greater the success or distinction will be (*f—f*—Plate VII.).

I consider it is far more accurate and less misleading to class this line as relating to brilliancy and success, as its name implies, than to call it—as many do—the Line of Apollo, or of art, for it is just as often found on the hands of those who cannot draw a straight line, and who do not know blue from red, as it is on the hands of artists, except in the first mentioned case, when it indicates a sensitive, artistic nature.

One of the best indications of this line is when it runs fron. the wrist straight up to the third finger, and is parallel to the Line of Fate and close to it. Such is one of the greatest promises, with, of course, a good Fate Line, of exceptional success in whatever career engages the attention of such a subject. For good examples of this see the hands of Madame Sarah Bernhardt and Lord Leighton.*

Do not make the mistake that a heavily marked Sun Line running from Luna up to the third finger is the same thing. Far from it in such a position ; it simply means a most eventful life, full of changes and uncertainties—but if such a line comes into the hand, and then runs parallel with the Line of Fate from that Mount out, such a career will become fortunate and successful.

This Line on Luna as above, although it indicates a bright, happy disposition, yet indicates the grave fault with the person's nature, that they are themselves changeable—with men, moods, and things, they generally desire glory and distinction, but they have little continuity of purpose, and can seldom carry out their plans (g—g—Plate VIII.).

The Line of Sun may be found with a wretched, unfortunate Line of Fate, and if so, it denotes that the subject will always appear bright, happy, and joyous, in spite of adverse fate, continual sorrows, and disappointments.

The Line of Sun from the Mount of Luna, on an exceptionally well-marked hand, can promise success

* See Cheiro's " Language of the Hand " (Plates XXVII. and XLI.).

and distinction, but, it will be observed, dependent largely upon the fancies and caprices of others ; in this case, it is never a certain sign of success, being so much influenced by the fortunes of others; besides, the fancies of others must at best be a changeable quicksand, upon which one builds with no sure foundation.

Rising from the Plain of Mars, the Line of Sun denotes success after great difficulties, but whenever it rises and runs on straight to its own finger, it is favourable (*v—v*—Plate VI.).

Rising only from the Line of Head, and from that out good, it promises success from about middle life, but due alone to the subject's own brain work.

From the Line of Heart, if well marked, it simply promises that success will come very late in life. The Line of Sun should be clear and straight from the Heart Line out. If it is, it denotes that one's advanced years will be happy, and at least fairly fortunate; if there is no line, or only a series of little scratches, it foretells a most gloomy outlook for one's declining years.

When the third finger is much longer than the first, and almost equal in length to the second, a Line of Sun more powerful than the Fate Line with such a combination, denotes the gambling tendencies—but with everything—talents, riches, and even with risks of life. Again, with such a combination, a sloping Head Line generally goes with gambling, betting, risky speculations, etc.

A good Fate and Sun Line parallel to one another with a straight Line of Head is one of the greatest signs of the acquisition of wealth, the straight Head Line showing a thoroughly practical nature, and the other lines great good fortune in all things attempted.

Many lines on the Mount of the Sun show too many things attempted—multiplicity of ideas will in such a case interfere with all genuine success.

A star on the Line of Sun is perhaps the very finest sign of brilliancy and glory that can be found.

A square on this line is a sign of preservation to one's name, reputation or position.

An island, loss of position, and general misfortune as long as the mark lasts. Once past the middle of the island in every case things begin to improve.

When the Line of Sun can be seen a certain distance up the hand, but fades out for a time, and then renews itself again, in such a case the subject will go through great sorrows, darkness, figuratively speaking, but when the line is seen again from that out, brightness will be restored.

On a hollow hand, the Line of Sun loses all power, but denotes a bright disposition, and great hopefulness of spirits in spite of the misfortunes indicated by the hollowness of the palm, and it should always be remembered that a hollow palm generally goes with very poor health.

The complete absence of this Line of Sun on an otherwise talented and artistic hand is sometimes found, and although it does not promise that such persons never attain to fame or distinction, yet it indicates that such people, no matter how hard they work, find the recognition of the world hard to gain. Such persons have their coffins covered with wreaths, whereas in life they probably found it difficult to get enough to eat.

If the Line of Sun goes to Saturn, instead of the third finger, it is not nearly so good in any of its indications, it denotes that sorrow and fatalities will always militate against the success of such a subject; such persons may gain much, but rarely, if ever, happiness. If the line crosses Saturn or even sends a strong branch towards Jupiter, success will lie chiefly in positions of great responsibility and power, and in the management of people (g—g—Plate VII.). This sign is not, however, quite as powerful as the Line of Fate going to Jupiter.

CHAPTER XVI

THE LINE OF HEALTH, OR THE HEPATICA

Some flowers are bruised that they may be more sweet,
And some lie broken 'neath the rush of feet ;
And some are worn awhile, then tossed aside,
Some deck the dead, while others grace the bride :
    And so in Life, I've seen the saddest face,
    The broken flower, give forth the sweetest grace.
                                        CHEIRO.

A GOOD deal of discussion amongst students often arises as to where the Line of Health really commences. My theory, and it is one I have proved correct by watching the growth of the line on children's hands, and in cases of illnesses, goes to show that it rises on the base of, or on the face of the Mount of Mercury, and as it goes down the hand and strikes or approaches the Line of Life, so does it show the development of the illness, the dangerous place in life, and so forth. It must also be remembered that the Line of Life only relates to the length of life from natural causes —the hereditary length or shortness, etc., whereas the Line of Health shows the varying conditions of the health with greater exactness.

The Line of Health (Frontis.), if found at all, should lie straight down the hand, or at least run ιff at the wrist without touching the Line of Life in any place.

The less of this Line of Health, the better for the person. When it is completely absent the constitution is stronger, and even if the Life Line be ragged and bad, the person has a greater chance of recovery than when the Health Line is visible. The heavier the line the more the nervous system is impaired. When the Line of Life and Health Line meet, if one is equal in weight to the other, where such a meeting-place occurs will be in the greatest probability the point of death (*ſ—ſ*—Plate VI.).

When it touches the Line of Life at any point it denotes some agency at work undermining the life.

When a branch leaves the Line of Health and cuts the Line of Life, if the latter be poorly marked or have an island at this place of meeting, such a mark at least threatens death, and if found in both hands it is hardly likely the person will recover.

When found only rising from the Line of Heart under Mercury, and broad where it strikes the Line of Life, it denotes weak action of the heart if the nails have no moons, or if the moons are, on the contrary, abnormally large, it then foreshadows palpitation of the heart and finally heart disease.

Very red in colour with very small flat nails, it denotes nervous diseases which affect the heart.

When bright red and heavy in small spots, it shows a tendency for fever in the system ; the slightest little excitement will cause the temperature of such subjects to rise rapidly.

When twisted and irregular—biliousness, liver complaints and kidney trouble (*h—h*—Plate VII.)

When in little broken-up pieces—bad digestion.

In little islands with long, filbert nails—danger to chest and lungs (*see* Nails, Plate V.).

The same indication with broad nails—throat troubles (*see* Nails, Plate V.).

When heavily marked from the heart to the head, and red in colour—danger of apoplexy, brain fever, etc.

This, with what I have said in Chapter XI. about illness shown on the Line of Life, will give the student a good foundation and at least accurate information as to what is one of the most important points as regards the hand. The mark of illness or death need not be final unless the subject persist in following the course which is bringing such an event to pass ; seeing what the cause is, whether it be a tendency towards heart disease or a breaking down of the nervous system, is the province of the student of this study, and the greatest good may be done by the warning, even if the apparently healthy-looking subject should, for the time being, laugh at the advice.

CHAPTER XVII

INDICATIONS OF MARRIAGE

What matter if " the words " are said,
The license paid—they are not wed :
Unless love link each heart to heart,
'Twere better keep those lives apart.
                                        CHEIRO.

IN my larger work I have given this point a great
deal of consideration, and I am glad to say that
I have been so far rewarded by the many
letters I have received from students and others
who have been grateful for the information which no
other writer on the subject has imparted. In this
work, though all must be condensed, I shall endeavour
to make my explanations as clear as possible.

There are three systems which I use, and I cannot
impress too strongly on the student that it will be
necessary to learn the three thoroughly before
accuracy can be expected. If all natures were alike,
then undoubtedly one system might be used with
success, but as marriage is one of those experiences
which must affect every nature after its kind, it
makes it one of the most difficult points to decipher
in the majority of cases.

If the reader should ask why marriage should in

one case be more marked on Venus, and in another on the Line of Destiny, I answer that it is only reasonable that it should be so, for does it not follow that with some temperaments marriage will have the chief influence on their career, whereas, with others, it will have its principal effect on the love side of the nature ?

There are some enthusiasts on the subject, I know, who will object to this statement and who believe that marriage is the be-all and end-all of one's existence, and that consequently it must affect all alike. But alas ! they forget that the human family is a very large and a very varied one. Morals are a matter of climate as well as of education, and that being so, we cannot judge through our own pair of spectacles in this matter. In spite of palmists or other persons, men and women marry according to their own way of looking at the matter. Some marry for position, some for money only, some simply because their fathers and mothers married before them, and there are some (and I believe they are the exception) who really marry for love. Now this being the case, it therefore must happen that marriage is marked on the hands in many different ways. On the square hand, I have found it chiefly marked more distinctly on the Mount of Mercury, whereas on the conic hands very often it is only distinctly and clearly marked on Venus, and so on.

It stands to reason that even if a woman is very much in love with her husband, if his marriage with her has altered her career, that then such a marriage would give its clearest indications on her line of career (the Line of Fate). I have seen in many instances only the line on Venus showing when the woman had married, how long it had lasted, and when it had ended, whereas there was not another sign on the hand that would have shown she had ever married. We cannot find out all the " whys and wherefores " of life's great mystery, but because we cannot, we should for that very reason try to fathom the laws of cause and effect that we see daily in action around us. The three systems must therefore be as far as possible studied together. The oldest is believed to be that of the Hindus, which consists of the examination of those lines that are found on the Mount of Venus running parallel with the Life Line, called the influences to the life. A few of the clearest of the rules are as follows :

The line that stands out clearer than the rest, running parallel with the Life (*k—k*—Plate VI.), may be taken to show the most important influence of the opposite sex over the person's life ; the nearer and evener to the Life Line the better it is ; if it is very clear and deep, but widely apart, it then signifies that the person one marries will be of a widely different temperament. If this line turns from the Life still more and divides into a final fork, it foretells separation, or divorce if the fork is distinctly marked, and a little farther fades out altogether. If it only turns from the Life Line but continues on, it indicates that although there may be disagreement at the date when the Influence Line turns inwards, yet the two lives will go on together (*i—i*—Plate VIII.).

If the Line of Influence goes into, or forms an island, it denotes that the person who influences one's life will get into trouble and probably disgrace (*b—b*—Plate VI.).

If the line breaks in two, it indicates the sudden death of the person (*h—h*—Plate VIII.), if instead of going from the Life Line, the Line of Influence turns towards and gets closer to the Life, then will the devotion of the person increase with years.

Some people have a great many lines parallel to the Life Line on Venus, some very few, but it is only the line that is closest to the Life, and that stands out clear and distinct, that is to be judged, the others also relate to those one feels more or less affection for, and may be judged according to their depth and nearness to the Life Line, and so on.

THE LINES OF INFLUENCE, TO THE LINE OF FATE.

A man or woman who has many fine lines rising up and joining the Line of Fate, as a rule is one of those persons whose destiny is greatly influenced by those they are much thrown in contact with. If one of these Influence Lines appears to be much stronger than the rest, the date at which it touches the Line of Fate, will in a vast majority of cases be found to tally with the date of the marriage (*j—j*— Plate VIII.). If the Line of Fate is shown as an improvement after this point, it then indicates that the marriage has had a favourable influence on the destiny, but if the Fate Line be bad afterwards, it has had the reverse effect.

If the Line of Sun springs into existence **from**

where the Influence Line and the fate meet, marriage in such a case would bring position, happiness, and wealth.

A wealthy or powerful union is thus often clearly shown when this strong Influence Line joins the Line of Fate, and particularly so when it is seen continuing as a fine line by the side of the destiny (*k—k*—Plate VIII.).

When, however, the line is seen first rising straight on the Mount of Luna, then suddenly crossing over and joining the Fate Line, the marriage is generally one more of capricious fancy than of real affection (*m—m*—Plate VII.).

When the Line of Marriage appears to be stronger and deeper than the subject Line of Fate, then the person the subject marries will have greater power in life, and a much stronger individuality than the subject.

The happiest mark of marriage on the Line of Fate is when the Influence Line lies close to the Fate Line, and runs on evenly with it (*k—k*—Plate VIII.).

Some Fate Lines seem to yield or slightly change in course when the Influence Line joins it, denoting the great power such an influence will have over the subject at that date.

An Influence Line to the Fate deeply marked on the left hand and not on the right, denotes that the love has been more on the subject's side than on the part of the person who influences them. If the line appears on both hands it is a greater sign of the equalness of the affection, and a more certain sign or marriage.

If the Influence Line approaches but does not join

the Fate Line, the attachment at that date will be broken off (*i*—*i*—Plate VII.).

These lines are generally called the Marriage Lines, and form the third system, and the only one that is known to the majority of Palmists (Frontis.).

The deep, heavy lines are the only ones that are worth being considered ; the minor lines have very little meaning, except sometimes marriage contemplated.

The Line of Marriage on the Mount of Mercury should be straight and clear, without breaks, islands, or irregularities of any kind. When it curves or droops downwards towards and into the Line of Heart it foretells that the person with whom the subject is married will die first (*l*—Plate VI.).

When the line curves upwards the possessor is not likely to marry at any time (*l*—Plate VIII.).

When the Line of Marriage is distinct, but with little hair lines dropping from it towards the Heart Line, it tells of trouble and worry in marriage, brought on through the ill-health of one of the marriage partners.

When the curve downwards is sharp or acute, the person the subject is married to will die suddenly. When the curve is obtuse, gradual ill-health will cause the end.

An island in the middle of the Marriage Line denotes a separation for the same being (*j*—Plate VII.).

When the line divides at the end into a drooping

fork sloping towards the centre of the hand, it threatens judicial separation, or divorce (*m*—Plate VI.) the more it crosses into the hand, especially so if a line from it cross the hand into the Plain of Mars, or Mount of Mars (*n*—*n*—Plate VI.).

When the Line of Marriage is broken in two pieces, it denotes a break in the married life, but not necessarily judicial separation.

When full of little islands, and forked, it foretells great unhappiness in married life.

These three systems, if used together, will enable the student by practice to gain the greatest accuracy, either in the reading of the past, or the deciphering of the " shadows of the future." Instead of these three systems contradicting one another, they will be found to assist in throwing light on points one could not decipher with one system alone. One hand may show the particulars of the marriage clearly on the Mount of Mercury, another on Venus, and another on the Line of Fate, but the comparison of these three points alone will give accuracy.

CHAPTER XVIII

CHILDREN

. . . . So oft to bear,
Thro' early hours, thro' later years,
The story of a mother's tears,
Or of a father's drunken care,
        Ah me! how hard,
To bear that load, that heavy cross,
To stagger on, and stumbling find,
All life but death, all death but loss,
With eyes alone to virtue blind.
                        CHEIRO.

THE lines relating to children are the fine, upright lines from the middle or end of the Line of Marriage on the Mount of Mercury (*o*—Plate VI.). By the position of these lines, where they end, and how they end, one would be able to accurately make out the number of the children, whether they will play an important part in life, and so on.

The simplest rules to follow are :—

Deeply marked lines denote male children, faintly marked, females. Male children as a general rule are more marked on the mother's hand, while on the father's hand the girls may be more often seen. Clear lines denote strong, healthy children, wavy lines the reverse. When the first part is marked as a little island, the child will be delicate in early life ; if it be well marked farther it will grow out of ill-health.

If found ending at the island, death will be the result (*k*—Plate VII.). When a line appears clearer and superior to all the rest, one of the children will be more important to the parent.

Sometimes these lines of children will be found growing upward from the Line of Heart, and not from the Marriage Line—in such a case it indicates an intense love for children, and a greater desire for them.

The numbers are counted from the outside or middle of the Marriage Line in towards the hand.

On a man's hand they are sometimes just as clear as on a woman's, but this is rare, and only where the man is found to have an intense love for children and an extremely affectionate disposition. Again, sometimes a woman will have more births than the number of children marked ; in such a case only the numbers that are clearly marked, it is probable, will grow up, or at all events influence her in later years.

CHAPTER XIX

THE VIA LASCIVA AND THE LINE OF INTUITION

THE Via Lasciva (Frontis.) is very often confounded with the Health Line, as its position on the hand is extremely close to the latter ; it is, however, a very distinct *curved* mark, but one that is not very often found.

It may generally be noticed as a bright red, broad looking line, rising like a loop at the base or middle of Luna, and running straight across into Venus on the opposite side ; in such a way, it is a most unfavourable mark to have ; it denotes lascivious imaginations that generally shorten the life by giving greater indulgence to the passions. If found running off into the wrist it is far less dangerous.

I have often noticed it on the hands of drunkards, and also persons addicted to morphine, opium, and such drugs.

THE LINE OF INTUITION

The Line of Intuition (Frontis.) is also **very** seldom found. Its position on the hand is that of **a** semi-circle from the Mount of Mercury to that of Luna ; it sometimes runs through or is partly mixed up with the Hepatica, but in good cases can be found perfectly clear and distinct, even when a Hepatica is also on the hand. It denotes a more than usually impressionable nature, a person keenly sensitive to surroundings and influence of all kinds, a "sensitive" in every respect.

CHAPTER XX

THE GIRDLE OF VENUS, THE RING OF SATURN, AND THE THREE BRACELETS

THE Girdle of Venus (Frontis.) I have never found to indicate that sensuality that is so generally ascribed to it by most writers, except when it is found on a short, thickset hand, with the rest of the signs bad ; it is usually found on such hands as the philosophic, conic, or psychic.

It denotes a highly strung, sensitive temperament, a person rather changeable in moods, and easily offended over little things.

If unbroken, it gives a most unhappy tendency towards hysteria and despondency.

When the Girdle goes over the side of the hand, and by doing so comes in contact with the Line of Marriage, it generally destroys the happiness of the marriage, through exacting too much attention from the person the subject is united to (m—m—Plate VIII.).

THE RING OF SATURN

The Ring of Saturn (Frontis.) is a most unfortunate sign to have ; it seems to cut off the Mount of

Fate in such a way that such people never seem to gain anything they work or strive for. Their temperaments may account for this in a measure, as they seldom have continuity of purpose, and generally give up half-way.

THE THREE BRACELETS

The Three Bracelets (Frontis.) I do not consider of much importance, except as a help in classifying certain conditions of health, for if the bracelets are well formed and even, the constitution is good and they promise good health; when much broken up, the reverse. There is one point, however, very important, viz. :—When the first bracelet (the one nearest the hand) rises into the palm like an arch, it threatens danger in the bearing of children, and also general internal delicacy (*p—p*—Plate VI.).

CHAPTER XXI

MINOR SIGNS

THE STAR

THE Star (*q*—Plate VI.) I consider a fortunate sign in all positions on the hand, with the exception of under the second finger on the Mount of Saturn ; in the latter position, it indicates some distinction to be dreaded. A person with such a mark generally leads some fantastic life, and it frequently is translated as a sign of a violent end.

THE CROSS

The Cross (*r*—Plate VI.) is the reverse of the Star, and is seldom found as a favourable sign ; it indicates trouble, disappointment, danger, and such like. Its only favourable position is on the Mount of Jupiter, and with fortunate indications of marriage this mark is still more fortunate, and even alone indicates a strong, deep, and happy love affair.

THE SQUARE

The Square (*s*—Plate VI.) is generally called the " Mark of Preservation," as it indicates that the subject is protected at that particular moment from whatever danger may be threatened.

THE ISLAND

The Island is never a fortunate sign to possess ; on a Fate Line close under Venus it generally denotes signal calamity—betrayal, etc., but farther up in the Plain of Mars, loss of money, worry, and annoyance. To the Sun Line, loss of position while the island lasts. To the Head Line, loss of intellect or injury to the brain. To the Heart Line, loss of affection. To the Life Line, loss of vitality. To the Health Line, loss of health, and so on.

THE CIRCLE

* The Circle, like the Island, is unfavourable, except when found clearly marked on the Mount of the Sun.

THE SPOT

The Spot tells against the strength of whatever line it appears on, on the Life Line temporary illness, on the Head Line a blow or fall, and so forth.

THE GRILLE

The Grille (*n*—Plate VIII.) is often seen, and especially on the Mounts. It indicates an uncertainty in the character of the subject that

* Note from Sir Morrier Williams : " When the lines of the right hand formed themselves into a circle it was thought to be the mark of a future hero or emperor." I maintain only when the circle is marked on the Mount of Sun.—AUTHOR.

militates against the success of the qualities shown by the Mount on which it appears.

THE TRIANGLE

The Triangle is one of the most favourable of the lesser signs. When found clear and distinct and not made up of the main lines crossing, it gives greater power to the qualities of any Mount on which it is placed.

LA CROIX MYSTIQUE

This strange mark called " the Mystic Cross," on account of the love of mysticism which it gives, is found between the Head and the Heart Lines (o— Plate VIII.). It denotes special talents for the occult, mysticism, etc.

THE RING OF SOLOMON

This sign (Frontis.) also denotes the love of the occult, but in this case it shows the power of the master, the adept more than the mere love of the mystic shown by " La Croix Mystique."

HANDS COVERED WITH LINES

The hands covered with fine lines like a network spreading all over, tell of a nature intensely nervous, highly strung, and easily worried. Very smooth hands show a person whom worry does not affect, but exceptionally smooth hands, with almost no lines except the main ones, denote a more or less phlegmatic disposition.

TRAVELS, VOYAGES, AND ACCIDENTS

Travels and voyages may be told in two distinct ways ; one by the little lines that cross the face of the Mount of Luna (*p*—*p*—Plate VIII.), and also ascend through the base of it up into the hand (*q*—*q*—Plate VIII.), through others by the fine lines that leave the Line of Life, and go towards the base of the Mount of Luna (*t*—*t*—Plate VIII.) ; of these the latter are the most important, as they indicate changes through life that are important, both as regards the change and the distance.

Accidents are marked as sudden breaks in the line, or as lines falling from the Mount of Saturn to any particular point. A sharp break in the Line of Head, for example, generally denotes an accident to the head.

The lines from Saturn falling to the Head or Life Line are often the easiest seen and the most fatal (*l*—*l*—Plate VII.) ; the line must be thick on Saturn, and very fine when it strikes the Head or Life Lines, to denote that it is a falling line.

CHAPTER XXII

TIME—THE SYSTEM OF SEVEN

THERE are many systems of telling dates by the hand, but the one I invariably use in my own work—" The System of Seven " —is, I consider, the most reliable and the one least puzzling to the student.

Every line on the hand may be divided into sections giving dates with more or less accuracy ; the most important lines, however, and those the most consulted in reference to dates, are those of the Life and Fate. Plate IX. shows the way in which these lines are divided, and that the line that cuts the Life at thirty-five years of age also cuts the Line of Fate at the same age.

The lines that form the two sides of the triangle shown by this system are those that intersect the Line of Fate at twenty-one and at thirty-five ; this part of the palm has been called from time immemorial the Plan of Mars, which indicates the battle of life ; according to this idea, after thirty-five the battle seems to be decided either in one's favour or against one, as the case may be. It cannot be denied that it is the most active portion of one's life, the foundation, it really seems, upon which in later years we stand or fall.

The student must, however, notice the class or type of hand before proceeding to make his calculations. The reason for this is, that of course there must be a very considerable difference in the dates given by a square hand, for example, and that of the conic ; if the student will bear this in mind he will reduce or increase his scale accordingly, but the same rule can be made a sure basis for all, namely, the line intersecting the middle of the palm if drawn properly from the centre of Venus to the base of the little finger will cut the Line of Fate in all cases at about the age of thirty-five, and having once found this point all the other lines will fall easily into their places. After a little practice the student will be able to make a mental picture of these lines across the hand.

The middle of the Head Line, under the finger of Saturn, also denotes about thirty-five, so if an island or break in the line be seen at that point it will be found to mean that at about that age such a mark would affect the brain.

The same way calculations can also be given by the Line of Heart. Under the second finger it may be taken to indicate from twenty-eight to thirty-five ; under the third, forty-two to forty-nine ; and under the fourth, fifty-six to the end ; the Life and Fate Lines, however, can be more relied on for accuracy as to events.

I

NOTE.—The term " System of Seven " has been, of course, used for ages. The divisions of the Life and Fate Lines into sevens by diagram (Plate IX.) has, however, been originated by me. I am forced to make this statement on account of unscrupulous persons in America who have copied this system and diagram bodily from my " Language of the Hand."

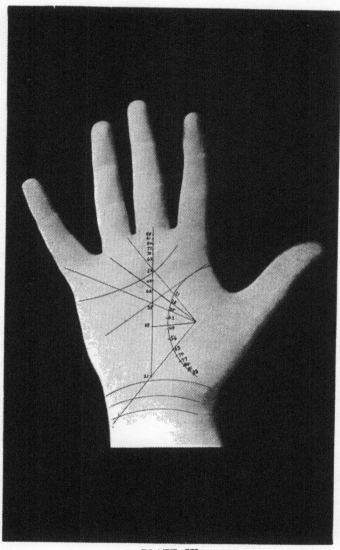

PLATE IX.

CHAPTER XXIII

MODUS OPERANDI

IN studying the hand I would advise the student to seat himself opposite his subject, and in such a position that a good light may fall directly upon the hands. I would advise that no third person should be allowed to stand or sit in close proximity, as a third person, no matter how quiet he may be, will unconsciously distract the attention of both subject and operator.

There is no special time absolutely necessary for a successful reading of hands, but the daytime is decidedly the best, as at night the circulation of the blood makes the palms reddish, and prevents the finer lines from being clearly seen. Both hands should be examined at the same time and on all important points such as illness, death, marriage, and so forth; the two hands should be carefully consulted before making a definite statement that this or that event is likely to take place.

Let the subject's hand first rest of its own accord on a cushion or table before you, and notice in this way the position it *naturally* takes, and what finger or part of the hand seems to dominate the rest.

When proceeding with the lines, however, hold the hand firmly and press the line till the blood flows into it ; you will in this way be able to see more clearly if its tendencies are to grow in one direction or another, or if little branch lines are commencing to shoot off from the main line.

Before deciding what these lines mean—mentally class the hand to its particular type, and remember that a square palm may have pointed, spatulated, or philosophic fingers, as the case may be, and *vice versâ*.

Note if the palm be hard or soft, whether the will phalange of the thumb be firm or supple, or whether it be long or short ; also see if the fingers are long or short *in proportion to the palm*.

Finally—speak honestly, fearlessly, but kindly to your subject. You can tell the plainest truths, but be careful how you tell them. Above all things, do not think that because you may have certain ideas on religion or morals, that those ideas must needs be right, and that everyone else must be sinners or outcasts because they don't happen to agree with you

Try and mentally *fit yourself into your subjects' place*, and strive to *feel* the effect of what their training, surroundings, and inherited qualities have been. If you do this, you will then be sympathetic, and you will take a keen interest in their tangled threads of life, to the complete forgetfulness for the time being of self.

Let your whole object be to do good, *to help the person who consults you ;* give him your utmost power, heart, and brain ; think of your work first, of self last.

Do not be discouraged if you cannot master this study in a moment. One cannot learn a language in an hour. Can this, then, the language of life, be fathomed in a day ? And lastly, if you do take it up, then take it up earnestly or not at all ; do not do it for amusement, or for some passing whim or fancy, but do it for the sake of the truth that is the foundation of the study ; and by bringing benefit to others, so will it also bring benefit to you.

SUPPLEMENT

SINCE this book was first published several very important points intimately connected with the Study of Hands have come before my observation, and as my sincere purpose in connection with this study is to be of assistance to those who are honestly trying to master it, therefore, in publishing this new and enlarged edition, I take the opportunity of placing some further information before my readers. For example, there are many scores of people interested in this subject who have written to me from time to time making enquiries as to the best means for taking impressions of hands, and for making casts, moulds, and such like ; and as for the past ten years I have received in connection with various points of interest in this study upwards of eighty to a hundred letters a day, one can understand that it is impossible, with such a correspondence, to answer as completely as one would wish the questions *re* casts and impressions that are frequently asked ; no more fitting opportunity could, therefore, present itself than the publishing of a new edition to give the desired information.

As regards the much discussed point, are casts

better to study from than impressions on paper ?
My own experience has taught me that the casts
have undoubtedly certain advantages, yet these
advantages are in many ways overruled by the ease
with which impressions may be obtained, and the
enormous numbers that one may keep without the
fear of their getting rubbed, broken, or discoloured,
as is the case with casts.

I will, then, deal with the art of making impressions
of hands first.

IMPRESSIONS MADE BY CHEMICALS

There are some dozens of ways by which good im-
prints of the hand may be obtained, as, for example,
there are many solutions of chemicals from which
one can get very good results. One of the simplest
and the best is that of tannin and iron.

To make an impression from this source it is
necessary to take a small portion of tannin, which
one can buy anywhere, and dilute it with water in a
flat dish or square pan. Take a sheet of smooth
paper of good quality and steep the surface of it in
the tannin and then hang it up to dry. When dry
the surface of the paper will become yellow, and is
then ready for use.

You next make a light solution of iron, brush it
over the hand, and then, placing it firmly on the pre-
pared paper, you press it for a moment, then draw
the outline of the shape by passing a pencil by the
side of the palm and fingers, and on lifting the hand
from the paper you will find a good black impression
on the yellow tannin background.

The great fault with this process is that the solution of iron on coming in contact with the tannin will also make the surface of the hand black, and it is a very difficult thing to wash it off again. In fact, with almost all impressions made by any use of chemicals the skin of the hand will suffer more or less, and that being the case, I do not advise their use for such a purpose.

IMPRESSIONS MADE BY SMOKE OF CAMPHOR

Blackening sheets of paper by smoke is a method that many people have employed from time to time, the smoke of an ordinary tallow candle being generally used. The impression of the hand is afterwards made fast by spraying with artists' fixitive, which can be obtained at any artists' material shop.

Although this sounds rather a primitive process, yet some remarkably good impressions may be made in this way, and with little expense or trouble, as after the operation one's hands can be very easily cleaned.

If other processes cannot be had at the time, the impressions made by the smoke of camphor can be very well relied on. For this a little piece of camphor, that one can carry in one's waistcoat pocket, and a few sheets of smooth paper are all that is necessary. Set fire to the camphor, smoke the paper, make the impression fast by spraying with the fixitive, draw an outline of the hand round with a pencil, and you will often find that a very good impression is the result. Most of the hands

that appear in my " Language of the Hand " were
taken in this way, and although some are not as
good as they ought to be, yet there are others that
are quite clear enough to show every line. I only
regret that many of the hands taken by this process
belong to men and women so famous that one
naturally would desire that the impressions were
obtained by the best means, but unfortunately I
had not always the best process at my disposal,
and had to accommodate myself to the needs of the
moment.

IMPRESSIONS MADE BY PRINTER'S INK

The best process, I consider, is one obtained by a
use of lithographic ink. To get the best results it is
necessary to use a small gelatine roller to roll the ink
on the hand. The entire apparatus consists of a
square piece of glass, a small gelatine roller, and some
lithographic ink.

A very thick ink, which is generally sold in small
tubes, is the best to use. Place a small portion on
the sheet of glass and roll it until the gelatine roller
will pick it up evenly. Get a block of wood so
planed that it has a slight raised mount in the
centre for fitting into the hollow of the hand. Roll
the ink carefully over the palm and fingers, place
a piece of paper on the block of wood, press the
hand firmly on the paper, draw the outline, and an
excellent impression is generally the result. The
impression of Mr. Gladstone's hand, which appears in my " Language of the Hand," was taken
in this manner by me on August 3rd, 1897. It

would have been still clearer only the day was so intensely hot that the slight moisture of the hand affected the ink, otherwise the cuticle of the hand would have appeared much more clear.

In order to remove the ink from the hand, use any of the good washing powders that are sold, and warm water, and in a few moments the hand will become again quite clean. Not knowing the means of removing the ink has kept back this process from being generally accepted, but by using the powder referred to there need not be the slightest trouble or anxiety about it.

To make the lines come out more natural, viz. : dark instead of white, as they are in nature, after using the above process there is a very interesting method by which it may be done, viz. :—

Take the first impression on very thin paper ; when the ink is perfectly dry, soak the side of the paper which has not received the ink in fine, clear oil, this will make the paper become transparent, and when it is dry one may use it as one uses a photographic negative to print from on sensitized paper ; this will reverse the lines, and they will come out dark, and exactly as they are on the hand itself. For those who can spend time in making their impressions they will find that this method is all they can desire, but for the ordinary purpose of taking impressions for reference and study the simple printing process is quite sufficient.

THE MAKING OF CASTS

The great advantage of making casts lies in the fact that they show the shape of the hand, but their great disadvantage is the ease with which they get broken, and the amount of room they require if one's collection should run into the hundreds, not to speak of thousands. Another point that those who advocate the taking of casts forget is, that the fine lines get so easily rubbed off the surface, and that the mere fact of even dusting a cast affects these small lines, and very quickly obliterates them altogether. Of course one may varnish a cast, and so, to a great measure, preserve it, but that is an after-consideration.

A cast can be obtained either by first making a mould in wax or some other pliable substance, or by making a mould of the hand in plaster of Paris itself, but the first method is by far the best.

To make a good mould it is necessary to get good wax, which can be easily procured in almost any town ; a special wax used by dentists for taking impressions of the mouth is extremely good for the purpose.

Place the wax in boiling water until it is sufficiently soft to be worked easily, form it into a flat piece large enough to receive the imprint, then place the hand firmly down on it and press it well.

When the matrix thus made is cool you prepare your plaster of Paris, and having first slightly oiled the mould to prevent it sticking, pour the liquid plaster into it and leave it to set. In order to remove the cast from the mould it is often necessary to break the latter to pieces, but this should be done with the greatest care or one may break the cast as well. When making the mould in plaster direct one must always oil the hand slightly to prevent the plaster from sticking. The matrix can also be made in gelatine, or even in ordinary putty if wax cannot easily be obtained.

DR. CESARE LOMBROSO AND PALMISTRY

The study of the Hand as regards the evidence of character and mental tendencies has lately received a most valuable testimony from the pen of one of the greatest criminologists of the century. I refer to an article which the celebrated Dr. Lombroso published in the *New York Journal* of May 28th, 1899. In speaking of the training of children, and the evidences of disposition and evil tendencies as shown by the formation of the head, the ears, the palate, the teeth, and so forth, this gentleman, the most acknowledged authority on such a subject at the present day, concluded his article by saying that he considered that for evidences of character and mental tendencies a study of the shape and markings of the hand were, after all, perhaps the surest guide. To substantiate his statements he gave illustrations of normal and abnormal hands with the abnormal lines marked. He paid chief attention to the Line of Mentality, or head, and his remarks bore out in every particular the rules that all good authorities on the subject have laid down for students of the hand to follow.

I publish this, as it is one of the best arguments that can be used to demonstrate to unbelievers not only the truth in the science of the Hand itself, but the immense advantage that might accrue to parents

and teachers if they could be induced to put aside
their prejudice and learn a little from that much
decried and abused " study of the hand."

I must, however, say a few words as to why, even
at the present time, in spite of the great strides it
has lately made towards public favour, this study
should be still open to hostile criticism and disrepute.
Alas, it is not the study, its philosophy, or what it
can tell people of the past, or their future tendencies,
that causes such a state of things still to exist, but
it is the crowds of so-called palmists that rush into
its ranks, and live, as parasites live, on the legitimate
successes won by legitimate palmists.

A little money to advertise and a good deal of self-
assurance are all the requisites that are considered
necessary. The public have not time to think, and
if they had there is not one in ten who would take
that trouble. They see the word " Palmist " hung
over some door, and that is sufficient ; they never
ask for the palmist's credentials, or his or her mode
or means of study ; they allow themselves to get
humbugged, and when they come out they turn and
rant against all palmists and palmistry, and yet they
do not know, as a rule, even the name of the impostor
that they have been swindled by. As an example,
in Bond Street, a short time ago, a man started as
a palmist, put no name on his door except those
attractive, much-abused words, "Scientific Palmist."
He had himself photographed to resemble me as
much as possible, and within ten doors of my rooms
for a short time he did a brisk business with people
who consulted him under the impression that he was

" Cheiro " ; in fact, he might have possibly remained there for years had he not engaged in blackmailing many of his clients, so that at last the police had to interfere, and the " place thereof knew him no more."

And now about this practice of blackmailing clients. There is no doubt about it that it exists, and exists far more largely than people imagine. I therefore cannot warn my readers too strongly to be careful of where they go when they consult self-styled palmists, or, worse still, some of those " mystery-mongers " who advertise Indian Occultism, Indian Palmistry, and such like.

In my recently published book, " Cheiro's Memoirs," I have made certain facts public about such things that were a surprise to many readers. There are some of these impostors who ask their client for their name and place of birth, so that they can consult (they will tell you) the Spirit of their Astrologer. For this information you will be asked to come back in three days or a week's time, and when you do return you will probably be surprised to know that you will have to pay about twenty-five, or perhaps a hundred pounds for this experiment, or else have certain facts in your past life sent in anonymous letters to your family. Never give your name under any consideration ; names are not necessary, and should never be required. During the whole of my professional work I never knew who my consultants were unless at the end of the interview, when at times they wished to write in my book of testimonies. Appointments should be made by numbers or letters of the alphabet ; this is not only the most straightforward way, but it also shows the confidence that the palmist can place in the study of the hand, telling the truth about the position and general surroundings of the client.

I shall be pleased at all times to give any further information that I can on the subject of making casts or impressions of hands.   Letters can always reach me through my English or American publishers.

." CHEIRO."

Lightning Source UK Ltd.
Milton Keynes UK
UKHW011159170320
360485UK00001B/24